THE LIFE OF OUR LORD

IS VOLUME

68

OF THE

Twentieth Century Encyclopedia of Catholicism

UNDER SECTION

VI

THE WORD OF GOD

IT IS ALSO THE

125TH

VOLUME IN ORDER OF PUBLICATION

Edited by HENRI DANIEL-ROPS of the Académie Française

THE LIFE OF OUR LORD

By *HENRI DANIEL-ROPS*

Translated from the French by J. R. FOSTER

HAWTHORN BOOKS · PUBLISHERS · *New York*

First Edition, November, 1964

NIHIL OBSTAT

Joannes M. T. Barton, S.T.D., L.S.S.

    Censor Deputatus

IMPRIMATUR

✠ Georgius L. Craven

    Episcopus Sebastopolis, Vicarius Generalis

Westmonasterii, die XXIV AUGUSTI MCMLXIV

H-9567

CONTENTS

INTRODUCTION

This little book seeks to answer two requirements. First, it was fitting that the editor of a Catholic encyclopedia should himself undertake the volume which must be regarded, from every point of view, as the centre of such a project, namely the volume devoted to Jesus Christ. This was the wish expressed again and again by readers not only in France but also in the nine other countries in which the series is being published simultaneously.

Second, since writing *Jesus and His Times,* the author has often received the request for a simpler, shorter, more accessible edition. "What we really need", wrote a missionary, "is a short life of Christ, easy to read and to comment upon, which could serve as an introduction to the reading of the Gospel." It was not difficult to combine the answers to these two requirements in one volume.

However, it goes without saying that there could be no question of "abridging" *Jesus and His Times,* that is, of making cuts in an already existing text. Nor could there be any question of "summarizing" it by trying to say in five lines what had previously taken twenty-five. There must be some harmony between the size of a book, its plan and what musicians call "the tempo". Something fresh was needed, with a different plan and a rhythm which could not be that of a big book of more than eight hundred pages.

Such was the intention of the author in writing this book. He has tried as far as possible to let the text of the Gospel speak for itself, seeking only to illuminate it and to assist in making it better understood and more deeply loved. Nevertheless, he has not refrained from using the results achieved by biblical exegesis since the publication of *Jesus and His Times* or from indicating the points on which his own ideas have evolved during the last twenty years. As a result, in certain directions the short *Life* of 1964 may be regarded as complementing and revising the work of 1944.

By its very nature this short *Life* is necessarily cursory and incomplete, but it will have achieved the object which the author had in mind in writing it if some of those who read it are led to continue their search for him who must always remain the only theme for meditation which never disappoints, the only guide and the only model.

D.-R.

CHAPTER I

UNDER THE IMPULSE OF

THE HOLY SPIRIT

The way was familiar to them: they had often taken it with him. Outside the city wide steps led down to the muddy Cedron; then, on the other side of the stream, the path climbed quite steeply up the side of the hill known as the Mount of Olives. Gethsemani was quite near, the enclosure of the oil press, associated in their minds with so many sad memories. No doubt several of them recalled these memories as they climbed the slope. But now it was to the top that he was leading them, towards the full light of the summit, to that airy terrace with its fine view of Jerusalem, amber and pearl in the May sunshine.

Who were they? How many of them were there? Quite a small group, no doubt. The eleven whom he had chosen and made his witnesses. The twelfth was not there; his body had by now been torn to pieces by the vultures. The passages which describe the event (Mark 16. 19, 20; Luke 24. 50–2; Acts 1. 9–12; and also John 20. 31 and 21. 25) give the impression that the band was a small one, consisting only of those for whom the mystery signified something more than a fresh and curious manifestation of an incomprehensible power. Many people have thought that the Master's mother was there too, sharing in the glory as she had in the abandonment. Perhaps the group also included those few women

whom love and faith had made so heroic that when the men
lost heart they alone had remained faithful.

When they had arrived at the top of the hill he stopped.
The others halted too and gathered round him. No doubt they
thought that once again he was going to address them and
pass on still more of his message. But this time he raised his
hand in silence and blessed them. Then a miraculous event
occurred. The Gospels report it as a historical fact, but it
transcends history and forms part of eternity: "And even as
he blessed them he parted from them, and was carried up into
heaven" (Luke 24. 51); "and a cloud caught him away from
their sight" (Acts 1. 9).

What heaven? What kind of cloud? The real heavens, if we
take the passage in Acts literally, the heavens above the
earth, the celestial sphere; and a cloud like those which the
autumn wind drives from the west towards the mountains of
Judaea. But we may also take the view that this was the same
cloud that a few privileged persons had seen twice before, on
the occasions of the Master's baptism and transfiguration, the
cloud whence the voice had come which Moses heard echoing
over Sinai, and the one described by St Paul as "unapproach-
able light" (1 Tim. 6. 16), God's sacred dwelling place.

However that may be, the witnesses of the event were struck
dumb by it. They stood there motionless, looking up at the
mysterious abyss above their heads where the Presence had
dissolved. A supernatural phenomenon, the appearance of
two angels, was required to restore them to a sense of reality
and of their obligations.

So ended for all of them the extraordinary adventure in
which they had been involved for about two and a half years.
Called by him, marked out by him, always in words which
made a private and particular appeal to the individual concerned, they had all followed him who had just disappeared
before their eyes. They had followed him along the roads of
the Holy Land which he had walked, taking his message to

all those willing to listen to it. They had heard this message, and it was so sublime and persuasive that they had been transformed by it immediately. They had witnessed the miracles which he performed so easily, and they had believed that this inspired man was "much more than a prophet", that he was in fact the messenger announced by Scripture, the Son of the Most High.

However, this splendid adventure had ended in what, from a human point of view, could legitimately be regarded as a setback. To the religious leaders of the Jewish people the new preaching had seemed both blasphemous and an attack on the established order; under the Israelite régime of that time the two things were in any case more or less synonymous. There had been a sharp reaction. The authorities had arrested the man who said that he was the Messias; a hurried trial had ended in a conviction, the Roman occupying power had acquiesced through weakness, and the mission of him who called himself the Son of God had ended on a bare hillock outside one of the northern gates of the city, where dangerous agitators, blasphemers and robbers were crucified.

This terrible defeat had plunged them all into a mixture of despair, apathy and fear. While the last act of the tragedy was being enacted, they were so afraid of being arrested as accomplices of the condemned man that instead of being present on Golgotha at the foot of the cross on which their Master was dying they had all—with one exception—gone to earth in the poor quarters of the city, barricading themselves inside a few friendly houses.

Yet a mysterious answer had been given to this mortal anguish and to the still more mortal doubt about the truth of the message which they had received. On the third day after the drama—the Sunday of the Passover—some women belonging to their group had gone up to the spot where the condemned man had been buried and had brought back a shattering piece of news; they had found the tomb empty and a luminous charisma had revealed to them that the man who had died on the cross had conquered death and risen again. Then, no doubt, curious phrases which they had heard on his lips in days gone by acquired a prophetic meaning. They recalled that he had told them that he was to conquer death after apparently yielding to it. But the very conditions in which for forty days this new existence went on had left these men in a state of mind in which joy, hope, anxiety and doubt all had a share. It was this strange second life which had just come to an end with a still more surprising event.

In the tradition established by those who were going to be the guardians and heralds of the Message, this surprising event was to have considerable importance. It was to be affirmed in the oldest version of the Apostles' Creed, which was a summary of their faith. In the writings of the first witnesses, this "ascension into heaven", this "taking up into glory" would be regarded as one of the surest signs of the divinity of him who had enjoyed it (Ephes. 4. 8–10; Heb. 4, 14; 1 Tim. 3. 16; 1 Peter 3. 22). For the moment, however, "the Ascension" did not suffice to dissolve all doubts.

In a splendid passage Lacordaire has depicted these men "alone before the world, which holds none of their beliefs, which indeed is totally ignorant of them, and which they must convert to their faith from the foot of the cross on which their Master perished. Was there ever such a moment for men? And who were these men? Craftsmen, fishermen. . . ." Their doubts, even their fears, seem only too natural. The task imposed on them would have made even apparently better prepared men seek to evade it.

Their faith was not in question and their hearts were "filled with joy". They could repeat to each other, as a sign and promise, what one of them was to write later: "No man has ever gone up into heaven except him who has come down from heaven" (John 3. 13). That was a spiritual guarantee which, coming after others, after the Resurrection, could not be denied by anyone. But for this faith to communicate itself, for their courage to rise to the point of making them take the risk of proclaiming themselves the witnesses of him who was crucified on Golgotha—a mortal risk expressly foretold by their Master (John 21. 18)—and for them to obey the supreme order which he had given them to "go out all over the world and preach the gospel" (Matt. 28. 16; Mark 16. 15–18; Acts 1. 3; 1 Cor. 15. 9), they needed more than human strength.

For ten days, gathered in the upper room—the very room in which they had celebrated the Last Supper with Jesus—of a house in the upper city which had become the dwelling of the first disciples, who had been joined by Mary, the Mother of Jesus, and the other holy women, they prayed and meditated. Those who had truly loved Jesus joined them there. The group was still quite a small one; perhaps about a hundred and twenty (Acts 1. 12, 26).

God replied to this confident expectation. It was the tenth day after the Ascension. In accordance with tradition Israel was celebrating the feast of Pentecost, the anniversary of the dictation of the Law to Moses by Yahweh. The devoted little community was gathered together in the upper room. It was then that the answer came: "All at once a sound came from heaven like that of a strong wind blowing, and filled the whole house where they were sitting. There appeared to them what seemed to be tongues of fire, which parted and came to rest on each of them; and they were all filled with the Holy Spirit" (Acts 2. 2–4).

There was no doubt in the mind of any of them. The breath of the Spirit which had just passed over them provoked a tide of memories. The Master had foretold to them: "I will send him to you. He will come, and it will be for him to prove the world wrong. . . . It will be for him, the truth-giving Spirit, when he comes, to guide you into all truth" (John 7–13). He had also added: "When the truth-giving Spirit, who proceeds from the Father, has come to befriend you . . . he will bear witness of what I was; and you too are to be my witnesses, you who from the first have been in my company" (John 15. 26).

So the moment foretold had come. The Spirit who comforts had descended on them. His presence made itself felt in their very behaviour and in the supernatural joy which they experienced, a joy so evident that the first witnesses—local people, pilgrims, inquisitive onlookers attracted to the spot by the strange celestial roaring noise—grinned at them and thought that they were drunk. But a curious power emanated from them and made them apostles, bearers of the good news, thanks to the mysterious gift which they had received of being understood by all who listened, whatever their language, and thanks even more to the fresh courage which lifted up their hearts and was going to ensure that even those who had abandoned the Master when he was alive would defend him now that he was dead to the point of sacrificing their own lives.

Proof of this was given on the spot. The leader of the little group, the man whom the Master himself had marked out as such, Simon, surnamed Peter, had been no more heroic than the others at the time of the great test. Recognized by the curious on the night of the farcical trial when he was waiting about in fear and trembling for news, he had capitulated at once and proclaimed three times—with an oath—that he had nothing to do with the arrested man. Yet—and perhaps this is the first miracle in the whole story—this frightened man, ready to deny anything to save his own life, a man, in a word, like so many others, found himself completely changed when the Spirit had breathed on him.

Rising, Peter faced the surging crowd. He was no longer afraid! He no longer hesitated! He would henceforth assume his responsibilities as a leader. He would reply to those who laughed at their joy, at their secret. And he would carry in his turn the message for which the Master had died.

Men of Judaea, and all you who are dwelling in Jerusalem, I must tell you this; listen to what I have to say. These men are not drunk, as you suppose; it is only the third hour of the day. This is what was foretold by the prophet Joel: In the last times, God says, I will pour out my spirit upon all mankind, and your sons and daughters will be prophets. . . .

Men of Israel, listen to this. Jesus of Nazareth was a man duly accredited to you from God; such were the miracles and wonders and signs which God did through him in your midst, as you yourselves well know. This man you have put to death; by God's fixed design and foreknowledge, he was betrayed to you, and you, through the hands of sinful men, have cruelly murdered him. But God raised him up again, releasing him from the pangs of death. . . . Let it be known, then, beyond doubt, to all the house of Israel, that God has made him Master and Christ, this Jesus whom you crucified (Acts 2. 14–17, 22–4, 36).

This precise moment marked the start of the Christian adventure which has now gone on for nearly two thousand years. The Church of Christ was to be born from this fearless harangue, which was followed by immediate conversions. Peter's witness summed up all the essential elements in the new faith. It was a faith which was not simply based on a doctrine; it did not simply demand adhesion to the teaching of a messenger such as Buddha, Zoroaster, Moses or, later, Mahomet. This faith consisted in full adhesion to a unique being, God-made-man, whom the believer had not merely to imitate or to listen to, but to carry in himself and live on. It was a faith which was to traverse the ages and to inform history with the mystery of Jesus.

CHAPTER II

JOHN THE PRECURSOR

It had all begun less than two and a half years before, probably in December of the year A.D. 27. St Luke indicates as much at the beginning of his gospel: "It was in the fifteenth year of the emperor Tiberius' reign, when Pontius Pilate was governor of Judaea, when Herod was prince in Galilee, his brother Philip in the Ituraean and Trachonitid region, and Lysanias in Abilena, in the high priesthood of Annas and Caiphas. . . ." (Luke 3. 1, 2). This profusion of chronological details, this comparison of dates valuable to the historian, is surely intended by the evangelist to show that this was the moment when everything crystallized, when the curtain went up on the drama. It was at the end of A.D. 27, then, in the reign of the Emperor Tiberius, at the ford of Bethabara.

The place is still well known today. It lies on the lower Jordan, not far from the spot where the river flows into the Dead Sea, that is, at nearly the deepest point in the Palestinian *Ghor*, that curious gash in the landscape caused by faults in the earth's crust. The ford is over a thousand feet below sea level and more than 3,000 feet lower than Jerusalem. In summer the heat is intolerable, but in winter, when the north wind blows, this unfriendly spot becomes delightful. The river has plenty of water and flows jade green between clumps of willows, tall reeds, mimosas and oleanders. The nights are like paradise.

A ford is always a busy spot. The caravan route from the depths of Asia crossed the Jordan at Bethabara. Long lines of donkeys and camels descended continually from Moab and then, after stopping to drink, started on the stiff climb up through Jericho to the Holy City. Thus people of every race, of every language and dressed in every garb had been passing this spot since time immemorial. But in the year 27 many of these travellers stopped. Others came too, from the various provinces of the Holy Land, attracted by the astonishing news which had spread from village to village: at the ford over the Jordan a prophet was speaking.

There was not a single Jew whose heart did not beat faster at the word "prophet". The story of Amos, Osee, Elias, Eliseus and still more of Isaias, as it is written in the Scriptures, was familiar to anyone born under the law of Moses and circumcised. But unfortunately there had been no more prophets for 500 years. "Our own emblems are nowhere to be seen," cried the psalmist, "there are no prophets left now, none can tell how long we must endure" (Ps. 73. 9). If a prophet really had arisen and was speaking at the ford of Bethabara, there were few who would not have felt impelled to hasten to hear his words.

The man was certainly what the word "prophet" might lead one to expect. "He wore," say St Mark and St Matthew, "a garment of camel's hair, and a leather girdle about his loins." This is almost word for word the scriptural description of the prophet Elias: "A shaggy fellow, with a skin girt about his loins" (4 Kings 1. 8). As for his food, that too was in the tradition of the great solitaries of the spirit, of hermits and ascetics: wild honey and locusts. The rule of the Essene monks expressly included grilled locusts in the bill of fare, and the Bedouins still eat them either crushed up as a seasoning or preserved in honey or vinegar. He had lived like this, so it was said, for years in the valley of the Jordan and the surrounding hills, retiring into the desert in the intervals when he was not taking the word of God to the crowds. If all this did not add up to a prophet, what did?

Since the discovery of the "Dead Sea Scrolls" in 1947 and the subsequent excavation of the monastery of Qumran, similarities have often been pointed out between the prophet of the ford and the monks of whose religious life archaeologists have been able to gain such a clear idea. No doubt the Essenes, ancestors in some ways of the Trappists, led a communal existence, governed by a strict rule, which was very different from the life of a wandering ascetic, but their ideals, their rituals and sometimes even their precise formulas were curiously similar to those of the prophet on the Jordan. It is therefore not impossible that the latter was connected with the Essenes and lived in a grotto in the cliff overlooking the *Ghor* like one Bannous, a hermit of the Hermon region whom the Jewish historian Flavius Josephus claims to have had as his master.

The orator of the ford was surrounded by an aura of mystery and wonder. St Luke the Evangelist alludes to it. Some thirty years earlier a priest of the Temple called Zachary, a wise and holy man, had been favoured with a charisma or special grace. While he was offering incense an angel had appeared to him, "at the right of the altar where incense was burnt", and had announced that his secret prayer was to be granted and that his wife Elizabeth, hitherto barren, would present him with a son. Amazed, Zachary had been bold enough to reply to the heavenly visitor that this prediction left him feeling sceptical, since his wife was too old to bear children. As a reward for his boldness he was struck dumb for nine months. The miraculous child had nonetheless been born as foretold, and, obedient to the archangel's command, his parents had brought him up as a *nazir*, that is, a person consecrated to God, chaste and ascetic, with his long hair tied in a horse's tail on the nape of his neck. When he grew up he had continued to keep the vow made at his birth: he had persevered in his vocation as a man of God (Luke 1. 5–25; 57–80).

He was called Yohanan or Yokanann—which we have turned into John—an old name with a divine root which was quite common in Israel at that time; it meant "blessed of Yahweh". But popular speech had given him a surname which characterized him more precisely. When you said "the Baptist", everyone knew that you meant the prophet of the ford. Baptism was his rite, his custom, a spectacular gesture which he performed over those who entrusted themselves to him. You entered the river, no doubt the prophet pronounced some liturgical formula, and you emerged supernaturally washed and purified.

Physically, the rite was not new; one had only to open Leviticus or Numbers to find the uses of legal ablutions. The *mikweh* was required of priests who ministered in the Temple and the rule of Qumran imposed a daily bath on the Essenes. But this baptism of John had a character of its own. One did not take the purifying bath oneself, one received the water from the hands of the master. Moreover, although the rite obviously had a symbolic value, it only assumed its real significance by virtue of the inward disposition in which one received it. It was "a baptism of water whereby men repented", a baptism of repentance. It was not so much the water as the act of repentance which cleansed the soul of the person baptized (Matt. 3. 1–12; Mark 1. 4–8; Luke 3. 1–18).

Repentance was the first great theme of John's preaching. "Yield the acceptable fruit of repentance", fast, pray, ask pardon of God: John was certainly a lineal descendant of Isaias, of Jeremias, of all the fearless men who had heroically reminded Israel of her obligations. As the monks of the Dead Sea put it: "God, with his truth, will cleanse the works of every man and purify him by the Spirit".

John's tone was by no means gentle. "Who was it that taught you, brood of vipers, to flee from the vengeance that draws near? Come, then, yield the acceptable fruit of repentance; do not presume to say in your hearts, We have Abraham for our father; I tell you, God has power to raise up children to Abraham out of these very stones." But to men of good will who came to him with the sincere wish to do better he gave counsel full of nobility; he advised them to abstain from all violence and any kind of hypocrisy, to share their goods with the needy, and so on. These words were the harbingers of stronger and more precise ones, for John was more than the Baptist: he was the Forerunner.

That in fact was the other great theme of the message delivered by the prophet at the ford. To those who asked him in wonderment, "Who are you? Are you the Messias?" he replied, "No, I am not." But it was written in Scripture, "Never does he act, but his servants, the prophets, are in the secret" (Amos 3. 7). Had he not been given the task of revealing to his own age the secrets of God? This question John answered in words that were both modest and confident. No, he was not Elias returned to earth, but nonetheless he had been entrusted by God with a mission of exceptional importance: "I am what the prophet Isaias spoke of, the voice of one crying in the wilderness, Straighten out the way of the Lord" (John 1. 23). For the supernatural being unanimously announced by the inspired prophets of Israel was going to appear: "One is yet to come who is mightier than I, so that I am not worthy to untie the strap of his shoes. . . . He holds his winnowing-fan ready, to purge his threshing-floor clean; he will gather the wheat into his barn, but the chaff he will consume with fire that can never be quenched" (Luke 3. 16).

St John has defined the Baptist's rôle in a few unsurpassable verses at the beginning of the fourth gospel: "A man appeared, sent from God, whose name was John. He came for a witness, to bear witness of the light, so that through him all men might learn to believe. He was not the Light; he was sent to bear witness to the light. There is one who enlightens every soul born into the world; he was the true Light: (the Word). . . ." (John 1. 6–9). It was a sacrificial rôle, implying renunciation and humility, and all through his life the Baptist was to be faithful to this ideal, content to humble himself in order to exalt him whose herald on earth he had made himself, him who was to come.

For a Jew of that time words and allusions of this sort had an easily comprehensible meaning which it is difficult for a man of the twentieth century to grasp straightway. In the Israel of 2,000 years ago there was an omnipresent sense of what the synoptic gospels[1] call "the fullness of time". The mysterious tomorrow was going to yield its secrets; the hour was at hand (Mark 1. 15; Gal. 4. 4); the event promised for centuries was going to occur: the Messias was going to appear.

Here again, to understand what this hope meant to a believer of two thousand years ago we should need a fresh attitude of mind, quite different from our normal twentieth-century one. We no longer feel in ourselves that upsurge of love which the Jews had in their breasts when they heard the words, "The Messias is coming". The Messias, the Lord's anointed, in Aramaic *meshiah*, in Greek *christos*, was, in Jewish tradition, the supernatural being who would arise when the time was accomplished to bear the definitive Word of God. It was of little consequence that there were differences in the way people imagined the coming of this repository of the divine message; the great majority thought of him as a conquering king, others as a master of justice and wisdom, while a shattering, enigmatic passage in the prophet Isaias (53) described him as a victim who would expiate the sins of men. The essential point was that believers lived on the expectation of this coming; a man who announced it as imminent was bound to make a deep impression on them.

One day, probably at the beginning of the year 28, there appeared in the crowd surging round the Baptist a man whom

---

[1] The synoptic gospels (Matthew, Mark and Luke) are, it is widely held, in literary dependence on each other: "they are clearly all variants of one single view or, in Greek, *synopsis* of the incident concerned; hence the description of these gospels as synoptic" (*What is the Bible?* by Daniel-Rops, pp. 86–7).

the prophet, thanks to the mysterious power which he possessed, recognized and identified instantly. The scene, as it is described in the three synoptic gospels (Matt. 3. 13–17; Mark 1. 9–11; Luke 3. 21–28), is a striking one. The stranger stands before John, asking to be baptized. The prophet is overcome by an uneasiness that he cannot suppress. He makes excuses, he tries to decline. With eyes which are not those of the flesh he looks at this unusual penitent and declares that he has no sin to confess or to do penance for. "It is I," he murmurs, "that ought to be baptized by thee, and dost thou come to me instead?" But his interlocutor replies, in a tone that admits no reply: "Let it be so for the present; it is well that we should thus fulfil all due observance." It is the condition of man to be a sinner, and one cannot be a man without needing to do penance; such is God's justice, to which even the purest man who ever lived had to give the appearance of submitting.

This fact has given rise to all kinds of speculations and not a few heresies. If the penitent of Bethabara wished to receive the baptism of penitence, said the followers of Mani later on, was it not because he had really sinned? And was it not only after the incident at the Jordan that he became completely pure, completely God's messenger? Other dissidents assert that it was only then that divinity descended on him and the mystery known to dogma as the Incarnation was consummated. These discussions are idle and futile compared with the simple fact which arouses so much wonder and hope in the sinner: the Messias penitent.

So John obeyed. The man entered the river and the prophet pronounced the words which he was accustomed to use. Later the baptizer was to bear witness to what he had seen at the moment when "all due observance was being fulfilled". A few days afterwards, indeed, he was to point out his astonishing penitent to those around him as "the Lamb of God who takes away the sin of the world", and as him "who takes rank before me; he was when I was not" (John 1. 29, 30), that is, as the Messias. In fact, at the moment when the stranger had emerged from the water and knelt down to pray, the heavens had opened: the Holy Spirit had come down visibly in the form of a dove and rested on the man praying, while a supernatural voice said: "This is my beloved Son, in whom I am well pleased."

The stranger marked out by the divine voice, the man before whom John the Baptist, in confusion, had felt his whole being dissolve in adoration, was known on earth as Jesus. He was a Galilean and came from Nazareth.

CHAPTER III

THE ANGELS SPEAK

The ineffable voice would have had no need to say that God was well pleased in Jesus of Nazareth if the marvellous events attending his birth had been known. But it seems that no one, either then or throughout the public life of Jesus, did know anything about them. We ourselves learn of them from only two of the four evangelists, St Luke and St Matthew. The two others are quite unaware of them. Moreover, in the first and third gospels, whose accounts in any case differ considerably, they appear as exordia or prefaces which can easily be detached from the body of the work. Nevertheless, the whole tradition regards them as just as authentic as the rest of these two gospels, and even heretics like Cerinthus and Carpocrates, or pagans like Celsus, who attacked the dogma of the Incarnation, do not question their veracity.

Everything seems to indicate that when the two "evangelists of the Childhood" compiled their books they enjoyed personal sources of information, those of St Luke being the more abundant and precise, and that they made use of these sources to add a kind of introduction to the material which formed the common stock of the Synoptics. What were these sources? If we read the relevant chapters of the two gospels we find that only one answer is possible. One person, a young woman, occupies an important place in them, and we are forced to note that she was the only one familiar with many of the events related. Moreover, St Luke says of her on two occasions (2. 19 and 2. 51) that she "treasured up all these sayings, and reflected on them in her heart", that is, that she did not speak to others about them. This woman is she whom we call Mary, the mother of Jesus.

She was a young girl of fourteen or fifteen, the age at which girls were betrothed in Israel. She lived in a tiny village in Galilee, in the bosom of a family which certainly belonged to the line of King David but was none the less modest and poor. There was nothing to distinguish her, as far as we can see, from the village girls of Nazareth. The name which this young girl bore, *Mirya,* an old biblical name which meant "Beloved of Ya" (Yahweh), usually distorted into *Miriam* or *Mariam,* was a very common word which was interpreted as "Good Lady". She was betrothed—this too was normal—to a man much older than herself, a cabinet-maker and carpenter called Joseph.

In the quiet monotony of the simple life of a young Jewish girl, occupied in the household tasks of those days, that is, not only cooking and mending, but also the kneading and baking of bread and the spinning and weaving of wool, a miraculous event had occurred, the one which, more than any other, Mary was to "treasure up in her heart" for a long time. One day when she was alone an angel had appeared to her. A Jewish child, brought up on the Bible, knew that these supernatural beings often intervened in the lives of men. Nevertheless, she had been extremely excited. The strange presence (a human form, a white bird or simply light?) had paused in front of her and Mary had heard its voice saying to her: "Hail, thou who art full of grace, the Lord is with thee; blessed art thou among women." What could this greeting mean? Then the angel had said: "Mary, do not be afraid; thou hast found favour in the sight of God. And behold, thou shalt conceive in thy womb, and shalt bear a son, and shalt call him Jesus. He shall be great, and men will know him for the Son of the Most High." Stupefied, the young virgin had objected, "How can that be, since I have no knowledge of man?" And the angel's reply had been even more stupefying: "The Holy Spirit will come upon thee, and the power of the Most High will overshadow thee. Thus this holy offspring of thine shall be known for the Son of God" (Luke 1. 29–35).

Where did this delightful scene take place? Thousands of artists have imagined their own settings for it: by the well, in the woods, in the Florentine countryside, on a balcony, by a Flemish canal. Perhaps we should visualize it happening, more humbly, in the bare kitchen of one of those mud-fronted cave-like houses still to be seen in the little villages of Galilee. If we think of the message to be brought one day by the child of these supernatural nuptials, then it becomes clear that the grandeur of the event is in perfect accord with the humbleness of the setting.

For Mary had replied to the angel. She had replied with total acquiescence: "Behold the handmaid of the Lord; let it be unto me according to thy word" (Luke 1. 38). Described by Bossuet as "the foundation of the great devotion which the Church has always had for the Virgin Mary", these words of Mary's hardly leave room for any commentary. It would be impossible to imagine a more total faith in the divine word, or a more absolute renunciation of human prudence in favour of the service of God. Mary said "Yes", and the greatest of all mysteries was accomplished: God's Incarnation in human nature. The event has more to do with worship than with history.

Human nature, submitting to the divine will, fulfilled its function, and as a result of the Holy Spirit's visit the little virgin was soon carrying a child in her womb. At this point another sign was given to Mary, in accordance with something else that the angel had said. His words had been these: "See, moreover, how it fares with thy cousin Elizabeth; she is old, yet she too has conceived a son; she who was reproached with barrenness is now in her sixth month" (Luke 1. 36). No doubt it was to observe the truth of these words that Mary set out on a journey. The trip from Galilee to Judaea, where Elizabeth lived, on foot or on a donkey, takes at least three days, and the village of Ain-Karim where tradition puts the scene is further on past the Holy City. The miraculous circumstance of which the angel had spoken was in fact the one which marked, as we have seen, the birth of John the Forerunner. Everything about this story, in which angels spoke to men, was supernatural.

When Mary arrived at the house of her cousin the latter was filled with the spirit of prophecy. She repeated the angel's words as if she had heard them herself: "Blessed art thou among women!" Then she went on: "Blessed is the fruit of thy womb! How have I deserved to be thus visited by the mother of my Lord? Why, as soon as ever the voice of thy greeting sounded in my ears, the child in my womb leaped for joy. Blessed art thou for thy believing; the message that was brought to thee from the Lord shall have fulfilment" (Luke 1. 39–45).

So all the angel had said was true. Zachary's wife, old though she was, was going to bring forth a child, and at the first glance she had guessed what child it was that Mary carried in her womb. Then, filled in her turn with the mysterious inspiration which had taken hold of Elizabeth, the Virgin who was to be a mother intoned a hymn, a hymn comparable to the finest in the Jewish tradition, full of biblical reminiscences, the sublime canticle known as the *Magnificat*.

"My soul magnifies the Lord; my spirit has found joy in God. . . ." Five strophes followed, all admirable in their inspiration, fervour and rhythm. They form a hymn of thanksgiving to the Almighty, who was accomplishing such great things through these two women, but also a summary of the message to be brought one day to mankind by the child born of the spirit.

Nevertheless, miraculous as it was, the event accomplished through Mary raised some delicate problems. Apparent con-

flicts between the supernatural and the earthly law are not a
purely modern phenomenon. Mary was betrothed to Joseph.
According to modern law, marriage alone constitutes the
final bond; breach of promise does not confer any right to
reparation unless there is scandal and prejudice. In Jewish law
the situation was quite different. The two states of betrothal
and marriage were certainly distinguished, and the latter was
only achieved by the "taking of possession", the *haknachah*
or "union" of the two people for life, but in practice the two
states tended to become confused. For a year in the case of
virgins the betrothed woman was placed "under the law" of
her future husband. Theoretically, sexual relations between
the two were not allowed, but the Talmud recognizes that they
did in fact often exist. A child born in these circumstances
was regarded as legitimate; that is why the woman had to
observe strict faithfulness. If she aroused suspicion, she had
to undergo the dreadful "test of bitter water": the apocryphal
Gospel of St James, which was widely read in the early days
of the Church, says that Mary herself was subjected to this.
If the woman was convicted of adultery she had to suffer the
penalty laid down in Deuteronomy (22. 23) for unfaithful
wives, namely stoning.

Humanly speaking, then, we can hardly be surprised that
Joseph, Mary's betrothed, showed some surprise. But once
again heaven intervened. An angel came to speak to the
husband-to-be, who was worried and doubtful of his future
wife's faithfulness. "Joseph," said the angel, "do not be afraid
to take thy wife Mary to thyself, for it is by the power of the
Holy Ghost that she has conceived this child; and she will
bear a son, whom thou shalt call Jesus" (Matt. 1. 20–21). What
splendid faith! Just as Mary had believed the angel's words
without hesitation, so Joseph in his turn surrendered to a
supernatural statement. He had thought of repudiating his
little bride-to-be, though "in secret . . . (for) he would not
have her put to open shame"; instead, he kept her, married
her and was to act towards her and her child as a foster-father,

a disinterested protector. There is something both sublime and touching about St Joseph, Mary's husband, this generous man "whose mere name", said Claudel, "makes superior people smile".

The months passed by and for Mary the end of her term approached. At this point a somewhat unexpected event occurred which was to involve the birth of the child in complications. An administrative measure—a census of the population of her Empire—was decreed by Rome. There is nothing surprising about the measure as such; we are familiar with many instances of a census. What is rather surprising is that the decision was applicable to the Jewish kingdom, whose master, Herod the Great, claimed full sovereignty. Either Rome imposed it on the little despots under her wing or Herod himself, eager to cringe to the protecting power, decided that the measure should apply to Judaea by way of a display of zeal.

Anyway, the order obliged many of the inhabitants of Judaea to make a journey. In accordance with customs still familiar in the Moslem world, the individual Jew was an integral member of his clan and everyone had to be registered at the place where his clan came from originally. Even today an Arab can tell you the exact spot where his family originated, just as Mahomet knew that his ancestors were Ben Qoraich's, people from Qorah. Mary and Joseph both belonged to the royal house of David, though by different lines of descent, so they had to be registered in the place of origin of the Ben Davids.

The place was known; it was indicated quite clearly in Scripture: Bethlehem in Judaea (1 Kings 20. 6, 28). It was there that, ten centuries earlier, Ruth the Moabite, who had come to glean in this foreign land, had won the heart of the generous Booz in one night of love. From these two, through their son Obed, the "tree of Jesse" had sprung, which often figures in the ornamentation of Gothic cathedrals; its supreme flower was to be Jesus Christ. In fact, a verse in the prophet Michaeas clearly confirmed the prediction: "Bethlehem-Ephrata! Least do they reckon thee among all the clans of Juda? Nay, it is from thee I look to find a prince that shall rule over Israel. Whence comes he? From the first beginning, from ages untold!" (Michaeas 5. 2).

So Joseph and Mary set out, she sitting on a donkey—the poorest families in Israel owned at least one of these good beasts—and he on foot, holding the halter. Either by the road through the valley, if it was winter, or else, more probably, by the one running along the crest of the hills, they reached Bethlehem in long stages. The journey must have been a considerable trial to this young woman about to be delivered of a child; the movement of a donkey is tiring and Herod's roads were not up to the standard of Roman roads. The disappointment in store for the travellers at the end of their journey was therefore all the more painful.

It seems that the bustle of the census had brought too many visitors to Bethlehem. Everything was full—inns, private houses, even the great "Khan of Canaan" at the gates of the township, a caravanserai built, according to one tradition, by a Galaadite, the son of a friend of David's. Even in this big quadrangular inn, with its open courtyard where men and animals were all mixed up together, there was no room left. The poor couple were compelled to seek shelter elsewhere.

St Luke's gospel says that when the child was born Mary laid him in a manger, that is, a receptacle for fodder; this seems to indicate that the event took place in a stable. An extremely ancient tradition, enshrined in the apocryphal gospels and confirmed by Fathers of the Church such as St Justin Martyr, asserts that the scene of the event was in fact a cave used to shelter sheep and cattle. Many such caves are still to be seen in the hills of Judaea. These more or less legendary traditions also speak of an ox and an ass as the only witnesses of the scene, a detail which would confirm the prophecy of Habacuc in the Septuagint version: "You will manifest yourself between two animals" (3. 2; the Hebrew has "in the midst of the years"). As for the star which we are accustomed to hang above our Christmas cribs, that too comes from the Apocrypha; no doubt it is supposed to be the one which, according to the Gospel, later guided the wise men on their way.

One can dispense with these sentimental details. The event in itself is too extraordinary to need any embellishment. A child is born in a stable, like a tramp, with literally nowhere to lay his head right from the start of his life, and this child is the one conceived by the Holy Spirit, the child of whom it was predicted that he would be Master of all, the omnipotent Lord. The Christian paradox is already there at the very beginning of the existence of him who was to take it to the world like a challenge. "When I am weakest, then I am strongest of all", says St Paul, echoing his Master. The child of the manger was to be stronger than any human power.

It was only fitting that celestial voices should make this known at the very moment when the child was born. For angels too were mysteriously associated with the whole story. An angel spoke to the shepherds on the hills, announcing that the child wrapped in swaddling-clothes in the manger was the Lord, the Saviour. A whole choir of angels took up the news and, speaking this time to humanity as a whole, repeated: "Glory to God in high heaven, and peace on earth to men that are God's friends." We can leave the exegetists and historians to debate on what precise date the event took place, and to decide whether it was December 25th, where a tradition dating from the fourth century places it, or in March or May as others have thought. The essential point is that this event, the greatest in the whole of history, took place unknown to anyone except a few humble shepherds and the angels, in the hush of "silence" mentioned by the Christmas liturgy, which borrows here from the Book of Wisdom (18. 14, 15), the silence of the world which alone makes it possible for the call of God to be heard.

CHAPTER IV

THE CHILDHOOD OF JESUS

Jewish law imposed on the parents of every male child the duty of having the little surgical operation known as "circumcision" performed on him. Whence came this obligation? From God himself, the rabbis replied, since it was he who had given this order to Abraham: "You shall circumcise the flesh of your foreskins, in token of the covenant between me and you" (Gen. 17. 11). The command had been obeyed for some two thousand years. On the eighth day the child was presented to the *mohel,* the specialist in this delicate piece of surgery. The Jews were more attached to this sacred rite than to life itself. "To be uncircumcised", said the Book of Jubilees, "is to belong not to the sons of the Covenant but to the children of destruction." It is very significant that Joseph and Mary subjected their son to the common rule: the human condition assumed by Christ had to be complete in every formal detail. Usually the circumcision of a first-born son was the occasion of great celebrations, but there is no mention of these in the short verse in which St Luke reports the event (2. 21). At Bethlehem this Galilean couple were far from their friends and their family. The entry of the Child-God into the community of the faithful, like his birth, took place in discreet silence.

It was at the time of circumcision that a child received its name. The choice was important; like all the ancients, the Jews attributed a sort of ineffable power to a name. According to one rabbi, a change of name made it possible to "avert the divine decree". The decision was made by the father, and it is worth emphasizing that, by telling Joseph that he should call the son born of Mary Jesus, the angel had acknowledged in advance Joseph's rights and privileges as a father. This name corresponded to our forename or Christian name; there was no family name in Israel; it was replaced by the formula *ben*, "son of", e.g. ben Zachary, ben Hannan, ben Joseph. The name given to the child was quite a common one; the historian Josephus mentions a dozen men called Joshua or Jesus. Four high priests had borne this name, and so had an ancestor of Christ himself. This too is not without significance.

But it was ordained that this complete discretion, this obscurity in the eyes of men, should go hand in hand with supernatural manifestations of glory. Circumcision was not the only religious ceremony which marked a birth in Israel. There was another one connected with the woman who had just given birth: she was considered impure, for forty days in the case of a son and for eighty in the case of a daughter. During this period she had to stay at home. Then, the time for "purification" having come, she presented herself at the temple, made a sacrifice and went off "freed from blood". When a first-born son was involved, this ceremony was accompanied by another, for in Israel all the first-born of living creatures belonged to the Lord (Exod. 13. 1, 2; 11–16). Perhaps this custom commemorated the "sacrifice of Isaac", when Abraham had offered God a ram in place of his eldest son, or else the lamb whose blood had protected the children of Israel on the night when the angel of the Lord had smitten the first-born sons of the Egyptians. At the time of the Gospel the presentation of the child in the Temple was accompanied by a holocaust of at least two pigeons and an offering of five shekels (about thirty shillings). Even the poorest people could not escape this obligation.

According to St Luke, Joseph and Mary complied with these regulations like anyone else. St Luke describes the scene in detail (2. 22–38), especially the two manifestations of which this modest event was the occasion. In the portico of the Temple, among many other people, an old man and an old woman were praying, witnesses to the fidelity of the Jewish people, which should not be judged by its priests, its Pharisees and its Sadducees. The old man was called Simeon and he was so holy that God had promised that he should not die without seeing the Messias. As the Galilean couple passed in front of him, carrying the child, the spirit of prophecy took hold of him and he uttered a touching hymn, the one which the Church makes her children repeat at the hour of sleep and the hour of death, the *Nunc dimittis*: "Ruler of all, now dost thou let thy servant go in peace, according to thy word; for my own eyes have seen that saving power of thine which thou hast prepared in the sight of all nations." Then, turning to Mary, he foretold her son's destiny, both his supreme glory and his terrible test. Anna, the other person praying, echoed this inspired outburst.

The aura of glory surrounding the Child-God made itself manifest a little later on in a more astonishing way. St Matthew is the only one of the evangelists to report the episode (2. 1–12): "And thereupon certain wise men came out of the east to Jerusalem. . . ." A star had indicated the miraculous birth to them and they had set out under its guidance. At Jerusalem they inquired of the rabbis where the birth had taken place. The rabbis were unaware of the event, but it was known through the prophets that Bethlehem would be the birthplace of the Messias. So the wise men went to Bethlehem and found the child, at whose feet they laid their presents of gold, frankincense and myrrh.

The picturesque scene lends itself to commentary and illustration. The artists of the Middle Ages and the Renaissance were very fond of it. The wise men were turned into kings on the strength of a verse in Psalm 71 which speaks of kings coming from the east to bring presents to the Messias. They

were given names: Gaspar, Melchior and Balthazar. Fathers
of the Church like St Justin and St Epiphanius—or Tertul-
lian—made them come from Arabia; other interpreters see in
them priest-astrologers from Persia. Even the "star" has
roused scholars' curiosity; was it a star properly so called, a
planet, a comet, a heavenly phenomenon or an astrological
conjunction? "A star that rises out of Jacob", said the Bible
(Num. 24. 17). It seems clear that the whole incident is primarily prophetic or symbolic in significance. This is apparent
even in the presents offered to the new-born child: gold for a
king, frankincense for God and myrrh for the body of a
mortal man.

The easterners' call at Jerusalem had not passed unnoticed.
Its ruler at the time, Herod the Great, had known about it,
had seen the visitors and had asked them to tell him where
they found the child. The plan he had conceived according to
St Matthew (2. 12–18) certainly fits in with the character of
the man as he is known to history: suspicious and cruel, the
executioner of his own relations. The mysterious child might
be a rival; it would be as well to cause his disappearance. . . .
When Herod realized that the wise men were not returning to
tell him what they had found, he had recourse to a decisive
measure, the massacre of all the male children born at Bethlehem in the last year.

However, the child escaped this "massacre of the Inno-
cents". Once again the angel of the Lord intervened and
Joseph had time to take his wife and child away. The Apocrypha have invented all kinds of details about this "Flight
into Egypt", and the Fathers of the Church have emphasized
its symbolical meaning. It was from Egypt that God brought
back his son when the danger was over, just as it was out of
Egypt that he had led his people. Jesus must have been between eight and eighteen months old when the death of Herod
allowed his parents to return to their own country.

They returned to Nazareth. It was there that Jesus spent

what have been called "his obscure years". For we know nothing about the youth or human education of the Child-God; the Gospel relates only one brief and mysterious incident. Yet how much one would like to know just how the transformation from child to man came about in this boy unlike any other, and whether the divine nature in him, with its universal knowledge, informed the human intelligence in a supernatural way! It is not surprising that the authors of the Apocrypha sought to satisfy the curiosity of the early Christians by relating all kinds of marvellous stories: how the child, knowing everything without having learnt it, routed the poor knowledge of his masters; how he changed a comrade who had hit him into a little mule, but then took pity on him and changed him back again into his original form; or how he amused himself by making little clay birds and breathing life into them like the Creator, so that he could watch them fly away. Pathetic miracles, whose wretched character was clearly shown by St Teresa of Lisieux.

The reality of the "Childhood of Jesus" was probably more modest. He lived with his father and mother at Nazareth, a very small village in Galilee. Some "independent" critics have tried to deny its existence, on the ground that it is not mentioned in any contemporary document, but recent excavations have uncovered the remains of houses dating from the time of Herod, and Avi-Jonah's map of Israel (1935) does not hesitate to mark a Nazareth in Roman Palestine. Like all Jewish children Jesus went to school, for since the great scholastic reform of Simeon ben Schebach a *beth-hasepher* or primary school functioned by the side of each synagogue, conducted by the *hazzan* or reader-cum-beadle. There he learnt Hebrew, the history of his people and above all the holy Law of God, the Torah, by studying Scripture. No doubt he also spent a certain amount of time in his father's workshop, handling the hammer and the plane.

Did he have any brothers and sisters? The constant tradition of the Church, to which Catholics are resolutely loyal, says that he did not, and maintains that Mary remained a virgin after his birth as she had been before it. Various passages in the Gospel (such as Mark 6. 3) would appear to contradict this, did we not know that in Hebrew and other Semitic languages the term "brother" is applied to cousins and even to nephews (Gen. 13. 8; Chron. 23. 21). In any case, as Renan pointed out, the expression "son of Mary", so often used by Jesus' fellow citizens, obviously describes the only son of a widow.

So the years went by. It would seem that there is nothing to be added to St Luke's beautiful words, "And so Jesus advanced in wisdom with the years, and in favour both with God and with men" (Luke 2. 53), which provoked St Cyril of Alexandria's wise comment that God, having put on a human body, wished it to develop in accordance with its nature. This discreet obscurity is interrupted by one incident alone, but it is an illuminating one. It is related by St Luke (2. 40–52), who probably heard of it from the mother of Jesus, for it is on this occasion that he notes that "Mary kept in her heart the memory of all this".

The child was twelve and was thus approaching his *Bar Mitzwa*, the thirteenth birthday which marked the entry of the young Jew into the religious community; henceforth he was a "son of the Law", and had to submit to all the obligations of his faith. That year, like all true believers, Joseph and Mary went up to Jerusalem for the Passover. The family had made the journey with a whole band of pilgrims, singing the fervent "Gradual Psalms" or "Psalms of Ascent". In accordance with the precepts of Moses they had eaten the lamb, with the sauce made from bitter herbs, and drunk their wine to the cry of "Alleluia". Then they had set off home again. On the evening of the first day of their journey back Joseph and Mary, who thought that their child was with others in the band of pilgrims, were amazed to find that he was not there. Their inquiries were fruitless. They returned to Jerusalem and after three days of anxious searching finally found him in the porch of the Temple, where the rabbis, the most famous doctors of the Law, gave their instruction. He was sitting in the middle of a circle of these grave personages, conversing with them: "And all those who heard him", says St Luke, "were in amazement at his quick understanding and at the answers he gave." Quick-witted and well informed about the Law as a little Jewish boy of twelve years can be—St Paul recalls in the Epistle to Timothy that even as a child he knew the Scriptures, and Josephus, somewhat boastfully, asserts that he knew the whole Bible by heart at fourteen—it is surprising that the learned masters of the Torah should have been so attentive to the words of a young boy if what he said was purely human in tone. The mystery of the presence of God in the man Jesus, which, as we shall see, makes any analysis of character almost impossible, can already be sensed here, in this charming episode.

The child Jesus himself seems to allude to this mystery when he replies to his parents' reproaches—legitimate ones from a human point of view—in these words, which were no doubt incomprehensible to them: "What reason had you to search for me? Could you not tell that I must needs be about my Father's business?" However, so far as our information goes, this was the only occasion on which he spoke to those nearest to him of the vocation which he knew to be his.

It was only when he reached his thirtieth year that Jesus emerged from this obscurity and started on his public mission, which was to last, as is well known, less than three years. There is something strange, something paradoxical, in the contrast between the two figures; it makes human haste seem all the more futile and wretched. For many years Jesus prepared himself for the task that he was going to undertake. For many years, as a craftsman and peasant of Galilee, he remained in daily contact with the earth, the work it demands and the crops it bears, an experience enshrined in his style of speech, with its strong, simple poetry which lends its fragrance to the whole Gospel. For many years he lived and supported his mother with the work of his own hands, by the sweat of his own brow, for this too is part of the human condition. The consecration of toil and effort was a lesson which those who followed him had to learn.

Then one day he knew that his hour had come, that the divine power which he bore in himself was to be made manifest before men. At that time Palestine knew that a prophet spoke at the ford over the Jordan. Leaving Nazareth for ever, Jesus set off to join him. This was decreed by Providence; it was not simply the result of an ordinary human decision.

CHAPTER V

IN THE COMMUNITY

OF ISRAEL

When Jesus was about to begin his public ministry, what was the situation of his country? Today we call this country Palestine, but no Jew would have ever used this name. No one true to the Torah could have dreamed of applying to God's country a term which would have provoked unpleasant memories of the Philistines, those enemies of Israel fought by Samson, Saul and David. He would have said, in accordance with Scripture, "the land of Canaan" or "the Promised land", sometimes "the Holy Land", or still more simply and nobly "The Land", the land *par excellence*. Normally people spoke of "the country of Israel".

It was a very small country, lying between 31 and 33 degrees north, and between 33 and 34 degrees east, with an area of about 10,000 square miles; in other words, about the size of Belgium or Sicily. From north to south, "from Dan to Beersheba", was about 145 miles; from east to west, that is, from the Mediterranean to the steppes of Upper Jordania, something over 90. But the landscape of this tiny country was quite varied. In the west there was a coastal plain, to the east of that a range of hills merging into mountains, the famous depression of the "Ghor", through which the Jordan flows to the Dead Sea, far below sea level, and finally the steep edge of the Asian plateau, with the mountains of Hauran and

Moab. It was a relatively fertile land (though we do not need
to take literally the famous biblical description, "a land
flowing with milk and honey"), a land of modest agriculture,
of pastures grazed by sheep and goats, in a dry Mediterranean climate shading off gradually into a sub-desert one. It
supported a population variously estimated at figures ranging
from 800,000 to 1,200,000 souls.

When Jesus was born, his people's country had been under
the yoke of Rome, either directly or indirectly, for about sixty
years. In 63 B.C. Pompey's legions had ended the domination
of the Hellenistic kings descended from Alexander's generals,
occupied the Holy Land and put a garrison in Jerusalem. But
this occupation had not gone as far as straightforward colon-
ization. At first the Romans had left the Hasmonaeans, the
heirs of the high priests, in control, then, regarding them as
incapable, had replaced them with a family of Bedouin origin
more or less converted to Judaism. In 40 B.C., a member of
this family, one Herod, had obtained the crown by the grace
of Antony, Octavian and Lepidus, the triumvirate then pre-
siding over the fate of Rome. It was he who ruled over Palestine when Christ came into the world; we have seen how he
welcomed the event.

This Herod was a curious character. In some ways he
deserves his nickname, "the Great". He had a sense of states-
manship, he knew how to place his kingdom in the most
advantageous position, and he was a patron of architecture.
But he was a tyrant too, in the most odious sense of the word,
a man ready to do anything to preserve his power. He was
such a savage executioner of his wives, his sons and his friends
that Augustus once said of him: "Better to be Herod's pig
than his child!" (for, being circumcised, he ate no pork, which
was regarded as impure meat).

However, when he died his kingdom did not survive him.
He himself divided it up in his will among his sons, the two
indicated by St Luke as the rulers of Galilee and the distant

provinces of Ituraea and Trachonitis; and the third, Archelaus, the eldest, whose share was Judaea, including Jerusalem. But if he had inherited his father's ferocity this princeling had not received his talent for politics. His relations with his subjects were so bad that Rome deposed him and sent him off into exile at Vienne in Gaul. His kingdom was attached to the province of Syria.

So at the time of Christ's ministry the country where he was going to be active was divided between two powers. Galilee belonged to Herod Antipas, the man whom Jesus was to describe as a "fox" or "jackal". Judaea was governed by a procurator from Rome. Since A.D. 26 this procurator had been one Pontius Pilate, a Roman knight, who would probably have remained quite unknown had he not been involved in the events which concluded the mission of Jesus. He seems to have been not very clever, not very vigorous, and extremely frightened of any kind of trouble, which is understandable when we remember that his emperor was Tiberius, who was always ready to listen to informers.

Relations between the Roman occupiers or protectors and the Jews were anything but warm. The rulers of the Empire distrusted this little people with its incomprehensible customs and beliefs, whose complaints reached the Eternal City only too often. The procurator was on his guard the whole time: for most of the year he resided at Caesarea, a more or less completely pagan town on the coast, but he kept a small garrison in the fortress of Antonia, which dominated the courts of the Temple, and when one of the big religious feasts brought crowds of pilgrims to Jerusalem he came in person to keep an eye on the situation.

As for the Jews, their ancient pride made it difficult for them to tolerate this servitude. They kept jealous watch to see that the Romans did not do anything that seemed insulting to their religion, such as displaying images of the human form. They disliked being subjected to the demands of the Roman treasury, which were rendered excessively heavy by the system of collecting taxes through "tax-farmers". To them, the Roman was not only the occupier; he was also the uncircumcised, the infidel, the rejected pagan, worthy of nothing but contempt. A pious Jew would not cross the threshold of one of these impure wretches for fear of soiling himself in the eyes of the Law. We must remember this state of mind, this tension which was always liable to provoke an explosion, if we wish to understand the climate surrounding Jesus' mission and, still more, the drama of his trial.

Yet the Romans had not interfered with what was most important to the Jews, their religion. Not only did they affect great respect for Israelite beliefs—the emperors sent offerings to the Temple of the Most High at Jerusalem—but they had also kept intact the politico-religious organization which the Jews had had since they returned from exile in Babylon. During their painful sojourn on the banks of the Tigris and Euphrates the Israelites had huddled round their priests. They alone, and the faith of which they were the custodians, were able to keep the scattered nation alive. Back in the land of their ancestors, but continually under the sway of foreigners —Persians, Greeks from Egypt, Asiatic Greeks, Romans— the Jews had preserved the same confidence in their priests and assigned to their religion the same function of protecting their nationhood.

The result was a curious administrative system superimposed on the administrations of the occupying powers, a sort of stateless state within the State. It was this religious community which constituted the framework of public life at the time when Jesus lived. At its head was the High Priest, a person of some grandeur, nobly dressed, very well housed, responsible for carrying out certain precise duties connected with the liturgy, and respected by the people. He was always a member of one of a very small number of families and it is doubtful whether he was much more than a tool in the hands of the Romans. Alongside him was the Sanhedrin, which was supposed to be descended from the Council of Seventy set up by Moses; it was a sort of senate, sacred college, supreme court and theological academy all rolled into one. More influential than the priests, who were confined by that time to their sacerdotal functions, the "Doctors of the Law", the "Rabbis", were the acknowledged experts on the Torah and therefore very powerful, since in the last analysis the whole of life was ruled by the Mosaic Law, which regulated not only morals and social life but also hygiene and other still more surprising sides of life. Such was the operation of a régime which the historian Josephus was right to describe as a theocracy. Special taxes, meticulously prescribed tithes, financed this system, to which Rome, the friend of order, granted her protection.

Jerusalem, the city beloved over all others, the royal city of David and Solomon which sheltered the only Temple of the one true God, was the capital of this religious, political and administrative entity. Pious Jews, wherever they might be, turned towards it to pray. "See you next year in Jerusalem!" was the normal greeting among those who lived far from the city. The "Psalms of Ascent" (Gradual Psalms) sung by the pilgrims expressed in fervent terms the Jews' affection for their holy city. People did not forget the sublime words sent heavenwards by their ancestors, exiled in Babylon: "Jerusalem, if I forget thee, perish the skill of my right hand! Let my tongue stick fast to the roof of my mouth!" (Ps. 136. 5, 6).

Well placed in the heart of the highlands of Judaea, Jerusalem was Israel's physical and spiritual bastion; it was also situated at a crossroads, a factor which favoured its development. Roads radiated from it in all directions. Twelve hours' travelling was sufficient to reach the Mediterranean. Situated where the central ridge of the Palestinian mountains ended in a plateau 2,680 feet high and severely eaten away by erosion, the city presented a noble sight. To anyone coming from the north or the west it looked, with its russets and yellows speckled with white, "like a stag", as the Talmud puts it,

"stretched out on a hill". When one arrived from the east,
along the road from Jericho or Bethany, the view was more
impressive still. Beyond the dark vale of the Cedron, where
the tombs of Josaphat's cemetery jostled each other, rose the
walls just finished by Herod, composed of cyclopian blocks
of stone and bristling with huge towers. Behind them the city,
dominated by the vast mass of the Temple, looked like a
huge topaz lying on a tray.

It was not a very big city. It did not deserve the disdainful
description of "hovel" applied to it by Cicero, but it was
certainly not one of the great metropolises of the age. The historian Josephus speaks of a population of 120,000. That is
also the figure at which we arrive if we calculate the area
enclosed by the walls. It was certainly not well designed, in
spite of the Jewish saying, "If you have not seen Jerusalem,
you do not know what a fine city is." Built without any com-
prehensive plan, with its narrow streets winding between the
houses, it presented the same appearance as the old parts of
the city still do today. Moreover, being built on two humps
separated by a ravine, it inflicted on its inhabitants the labour
of continually climbing up and down along its stepped road-
ways.

But it mattered little to the Jews that their capital was not
as big or as well planned as Rome or Alexandria. A Holy
City, the blessed spot where the one true God was worshipped,
to them it was above all the metropolis of the faithful, the
spot where the Jewish people could feel its heart beating.

For in the Jewish community at the time when Jesus lived
everything rested on religion. The whole of life was regulated
and controlled by it: the religious law, the Torah, made itself
felt not only in the sphere of morals, as one would expect, but
also in social relations, education and everyday usage. The
smallest gesture was accompanied by a benediction. Days,
weeks, months and years were all sacred.

The official religion was centred on the Temple, which had
been reconstructed on a grandiose scale by Herod. It was a

huge, monumental complex of intercommunicating areas, the
court of pagans, the court of women, the court of the Israelites, the court of the priests. In the centre, at the highest and
most sacred spot, was the sanctuary proper, with its Holy and
its Holy of Holies, the latter a mysterious place, completely
empty, entered only by the High Priest once a year for a
direct meeting with the invisible God. It was in the Temple
that the liturgical ceremonies were carried out each day,
notably the ritual incensings at the altar of incense and the
innumerable sacrifices of animals which made the sacred
building look surprisingly like a slaughterhouse. As well as
being the scene of these public ceremonies, the Temple was
also the setting for innumerable acts of private devotion, such
as those of old Simeon and Anna. From morn to eve its courts
were full of the faithful who had come to pray to the Lord in
his own house.

However, the Temple was not the only religious meeting-
place of the Jews in the time of Jesus. During the Exile the
Israelites had acquired the habit of meeting in groups to medi-
tate on the Holy Law together. These meetings—"synagogues"
in Greek—had continued after the return. Every township in
Palestine had at least one of these buildings where the faithful met to read and comment on the Bible; in Jerusalem there
were several hundred of them belonging to different quarters
of the city, to different trades or to Jews residing abroad.

The result of this intensive religious life was that the diver-
gent tendencies, which in modern states are reflected in the
formation of political parties, ended in Israel in creating religious sects. Two of these were particularly notorious. The
Pharisees put the fullest possible interpretation on the religious law; they "raised the hedge of the Law", were demanding in the matter of legal regulations and vehement in their
fierce refusal to have any contact with the heathen. The Sadducees stuck to essentials, to the written Law of Moses and its
613 great principles, but where the Law was silent they
claimed that it was permissible to act in accordance with the

demands of the age; they also tended to accept Roman occupation as a fact with which one had to come to terms.

The Zealots were religious and political fanatics; they were the revolutionaries of the period, ready to unleash rebellion against Rome in the name of extreme fidelity to their religion. The Essenes, on the other hand, were the reverse of the agitators; they probably included not only the monks—living as a community according to a rule—whose daily lives have been revealed in detail by the famous "Dead Sea Scrolls", but also a whole body of devout people, just as attached to the Law as the Pharisees, but less ostentatious, more genuinely motivated by love of God.

It was in this deeply religious atmosphere generated by a people different from any other that Jesus was to undertake his great work of publishing to the world a message consistent with that of Israel yet at the same time transcending it.[1]

[1] On the topography of Jerusalem, and other matters mentioned in this chapter, see Francis Du Buit, O.P.: *Biblical Archeology*, Volume 62 in this series.

CHAPTER VI

THE FIRST SIGNS

Djebel Qarantal, "the Mountain of the Forty Days", lies to the north-west of Jericho. It is simply a peak detached by erosion from the chalk cliff in which the mountains of Judaea end above the Dead Sea. A tiny Greek Orthodox monastery is perched on its slopes; it has only a few buildings and makes use of the caves inhabited by hermits as early as the fifth century. With its severe beauty, this desert site is conducive to mystical meditation. A vast panorama extends at the feet of anyone in retreat there: rolling hills, the green valley of the Jordan; to the rear, limitless Asia; to the right, the leaden expanse of the Dead Sea; and to the left, merging into the sky, Hermon with its snowy brow.

It was here that Jesus withdrew immediately after his baptism, "led by the Spirit", for a final period of preparation before his public ministry. These sacred periods of forty days were very much in the tradition of Israel: Moses had remained forty days on Sinai in the presence of God; Elias had devoted forty days to his journey to Horeb. But this particular retreat was marked by a very curious episode (Matt. 4. 1–11; Mark 1, 12,13; Luke 4. 1–13).

When the long, hard fast of the retreat had exhausted Jesus, the Enemy, the Power of Darkness, put this temptation into his mind: "If thou art the Son of God, bid these stones turn into loaves of bread!" When Christ refused, the Devil tried again; pointing to the horizon, he said: "All the kingdoms of the world are mine; bow down before me and they shall be thine!" This was followed by a second refusal and a fresh attempt by the Devil. Transporting Jesus to the pinnacle of the Temple—some three hundred feet above Cedron—he said: "If thou art the Son of God, cast thyself down! For has not God promised his elect that he would be borne up by his angels?" Jesus simply replied: "We are also told, Thou shalt not put the Lord thy God to the proof." Against the Son of God, temptations were powerless.

What exactly were the circumstances of this dramatic confrontation? Was it only in Jesus' conscience that this struggle took place? Was the removal to the pinnacle of the Temple physical or metaphysical? We can leave this problem to the exegetist. The essential point is that in substance the temptation which Jesus successfully resisted was that of temporal messianism, the temptation to use his divine power to impose a visible victory. For that would be the danger for those who followed him: the expectation of a kingdom on earth. At the moment when he was about to undertake his mission it was of capital importance that the choice should be made. It is significant that Jesus told his disciples about this episode, which was obviously known to him alone.

His retreat completed, Jesus came down to the banks of the Jordan again, probably at the beginning of March in the year 28. Since he had been marked out by God with a special sign and was henceforth completely prepared for his mission, it might have been expected that he would begin his work at once. However, several weeks went by, some three months in fact, which seem like a period of waiting. The full mission has not yet begun; what happens is more like a preparation. Jesus makes some gestures foreshadowing those which he will make later on, but with obvious reserve. Perhaps it was to let John the Baptist complete the task with which he had been entrusted, for it was only when his great voice had fallen silent that Jesus was to speak out loud and clear. Or it may have been to ensure that the sudden manifestation of all his power did not mislead those who were going to follow him by persuading them that he was going to re-establish the purely temporal kingdom.

The discretion surrounding the first acts of Jesus—indeed, throughout his life he was to maintain an obvious reserve about himself and his powers—is only comprehensible if we grasp the carnal and nationalistic nature of Israel's messianic hope. We should not be surprised that this hope did take such a form. It was only natural that this humiliated people should expect God's envoy to restore its power and glory. Jesus could have proclaimed himself the Messias right from the start and proved his claim by miracles and wonders. Confusion would have then been inevitable. "If thou art the Christ, tell us openly", his listeners were to exclaim (John 10. 24). Jesus had only too many reasons for not complying with this impatient request.

In the valley of the Jordan Jesus met the Baptist again. John had doubtless left the banks of the river and settled down some distance from the left bank, in Peraea. Prudence had dictated this course, for a delegation of priests and Levites had come from Jerusalem to carry out what looks like a sort of investigation. Was he the Messias? Why was he baptizing? If he was the Forerunner of the Messias, who was the Messias? (John 1. 19–23). John had replied with the same admirable humility which he had exhibited at the time of Jesus' baptism.

The Baptist recognized in the crowd "him who takes rank before me, for he was when I was not". He described him in one brief sentence to those standing near: "This is the Lamb of God, who takes away the sins of the world." The symbolic description, which was to be used continually in the Christian tradition, recalled at the same time the servant of Yahweh (Isaias 53) and the paschal lamb sacrificed for the safety of the People (Exodus 12). Two of those present trembled; they had understood.

The two were Galileans; a young man called John—the same who alone was to relate this episode in his gospel (John 1. 29–51)—and one of his elders, Andrew by name, a fisherman from the Lake of Genesareth (Sea of Galilee), where, in association with his brother Simon and John's father, Zebedee, he owned a small number of boats and nets. They followed him whom the Baptist had just pointed out with his biblical phrase. Jesus stopped and asked: "Whom do you seek?" Like two embarrassed peasants they replied with a question, "Master, where do you live?" "Come," said Jesus, "and you will see." The text of the Gospel says soberly that they did in fact go, and that they stayed with him, for ever. Brief though the words are, one senses through them that sovereign power of Christ over men's souls, a power of which so many proofs were to be given subsequently.

Andrew's brother, Simon, was not with him when John and he had met Jesus. As soon as they saw Simon again, Andrew cried: "We have found the Messias!" And he took Simon to Jesus. Jesus looked at the newcomer closely; one can almost feel the weight of his glance on this man. Then the call came, in twelve words: "Thou art Simon the son of Jona; thou shalt be called Cephas (which means the same as Peter)." The name must have seemed obscure to the man who received it; it would only be explained later, when Jesus told this Peter (which means "rock" in Greek) that he would be the rock on which the community born of Christ would be built.

Two others received Christ's call, two more Galileans, whom Jesus and his first three disciples met on the road back to their province. Philip obeyed one single word, while Nathanael was converted in still more moving circumstances. Philip told him enthusiastically that he had discovered the Messias—one Jesus, the son of a carpenter from Nazareth—and Nathanael replied with a joke. But when he found himself before Jesus, he doubted and laughed no more; one sentence opened his heart: "I saw thee when thou wast under the fig-tree, before Philip called thee." What was Nathanael doing under the fig-tree? What anxious meditation was he pursuing? The dialogue of Christ with the soul commands silence, but Nathanael too responded to the voice which called him.

All this had taken place discreetly, in the hearts of those concerned. However, Jesus was going to give yet more astonishing proof of his full power over things as well as beings. Back in his own district, he had gone to a marriage ceremony in the township of Cana. In Israel, marriages were the occasion of much eating and drinking. A marriage-feast could last a week. The Gospel implies that this particular one was a fairly sumptuous affair.

In the end the wine gave out. Mary, the mother of Jesus, noticed this and pointed it out to her son—a sign that she believed in him, that "the things which she kept in her heart" had convinced her for ever of the presence of the divine power in her son. At the entrance to the dining-room stood six stone water-pots for the ceremonial washing prescribed by Jewish law; they were big pots, containing altogether about 130 gallons. A word from Christ, and the water, drawn off at his command, turned out to be an exquisite wine, the best served at the banquet (John 2. 1–11).

Dostoevsky called this "a charming miracle". It was a foretaste of the supernatural act which Jesus was to perform much later on when he changed wine into blood and bread into the divine flesh. Did he do it to confirm his disciples in their faith? "His disciples learned to believe in him", says the Bible. But how discreet this miracle remained, performed as it was in a little provincial town, before a roomful of peasants!

However, it had not passed unnoticed, nor had the events by the Jordan. Jesus had gone up to Jerusalem, like the faithful Jew that he was, to celebrate the Passover, and he was surrounded by men claiming to believe in him. But Jesus maintained a certain degree of reserve, for "he could read men's hearts" (John 2. 23–25). No doubt he knew that they wanted earthly glory.

But one of them was of a different sort, and to him Jesus revealed rather more of what he was and of what he had to do. This man's name was Nicodemus. He was a member of the Sanhedrin, and thus one of the leaders of the Jewish community. There can be no doubt that he was an honest man and one who sincerely sought the truth. As he was a man of some reputation—and a prudent one—it was by night that he came to have a discussion with Jesus. He had heard people talk of him; he knew that Jesus seemed to have a supernatural power at his disposal. So he came to ask Jesus whether this power proceeded from God; that is—the question was a decisive one—was Jesus the envoy of God?

Jesus' reply was no less decisive. In the Fourth Gospel, the only one to relate the episode, it occupies two full pages and is presented as a long poem interrupted at two points by Nicodemus' questions, a poem composed well nigh entirely of scriptural allusions and almost word-for-word quotations. Christ disclosed to this man of good will what was to be the essential part of his message; the call to a radical transformation, to a "baptism according to the Spirit" quite different in intention from that of John the Forerunner. "To be born by water and the spirit", "to be born anew", to be made "from on high and no longer from below"; such is the condition for entering the Kingdom of Heaven. The whole message of Jesus is there, everything that is to be read in the Gospel.

But what is even more surprising is that Jesus makes it quite clear who he is to this stranger, this official personage whom he would have reason to distrust. He speaks of the Son of Man who comes down from heaven; he foretells—the phrase is a mysterious one—"that he will be lifted up" and that men will believe in him. He emphasizes that this envoy from God is not an executioner eager to punish but the bearer of mercy (John 3. 1–21).

The evangelist has not reported Nicodemus' reply. In any case, if he was won over by Jesus, his conviction remained secret. It may be that, like so many men, this member of the Sanhedrin heard Christ's call but, again like so many, did not

dare through weakness or human caution to give way completely to his enthusiasm and to respond with total acquiescence. We shall meet him again at Jesus' trial, speaking in his
defence, and, after the crucifixion, sending aromatic spices
for his body. Perhaps he was to give the dead man the faith
which he had been unable to give to the living one.

This preface, as it were, to Christ's main ministry was to
close with an episode possibly still more disconcerting than
that of the conversation with Nicodemus (Matt. 4. 12; Mark
1. 14; Luke 4. 14; John 4. 4–31). Jesus and his companions
were returning to Galilee. The heat was already oppressive in
the Ghor and they had taken the hill road, which was more
airy but in the eyes of strict Jews had one grave fault, that of
going through the land of the Samaritans.

There had been bad relations between the Jews and the
Samaritans for a long time; from the tenth century, to be precise, when Solomon's kingdom was divided between his two
sons. While Judaea, the little state in the south, had remained
strictly faithful to the Mosaic Law, the northern kingdom had
soon made a number of compromises with it. It was also said
that the Samaritans worshipped golden calves. In any case,
on Mt Garizim they had built a sanctuary in competition with
the Temple of Jerusalem. The epithets "impure", "soiled",
"untouchable" rose spontaneously to the lips of Jews when
they spoke of their neighbours.

While Jesus and his companions were going through
Samaria, he felt tired and stopped. His friends left him at the
foot of the hill of Sichar and themselves went on up to the
town, no doubt to look for food. There was a well there, a
very old well, known as the "well of Jacob", because tradition
said that the patriarch had taken his flocks to drink there. It
can still be seen, 100 feet deep, inside the ruins of an un-
finished basilica. Jesus sat down on the edge. He had no vessel
in which to draw water and he was thirsty.

A local woman approached. In the East, fetching water is
a woman's task. You can see women coming to springs and

wells, with a jug or tin on their heads or supported against
their sides. To this stranger Jesus said: "I am thirsty; give me
some water." The request was so unexpected that the woman
could not refrain from jokingly showing her surprise. She
must have been aware of the Jewish saying, "The water of
the Samaritans is more impure than the blood of pigs." The
two of them began a conversation which was to lead to a
curious revelation.

Jesus replied to the woman's mockery by saying, "If you
knew the things of God, it is you who would have asked me
for water. And those who drink of my water will never thirst
again." The woman was astonished; the words must have
seemed extremely mysterious to her. She replied by speaking
of the water of the well, the water that she had to draw every
day. Jesus repeated what he had said before. We can imagine
his gaze resting on her, as it rested on Nathanael and Peter, the
gaze which reached to the bottom of the soul. To be brief,
he unmasked her and told her what she knew only too well,
that she was living with a man who was not her husband.
She gave in, acknowledging that this man who could read
your heart was a prophet.

It was at this point that Jesus disclosed to this woman of
no account, this heretic, both the essentials of his message
and the truth about himself. The time was approaching, he
said, when both Samaritans and Jews would be called to
worship God no longer in a temple, but in spirit and truth, in
their inmost hearts. And when the woman said, "Yes, I know,
the things of which you speak will be accomplished when the
Messias comes", he replied, "I who speak to you am
the Messias." Why did he communicate to this alien woman
a secret which he had never yet shared with anyone, a
secret which he was to guard closely all through his life? Precisely because she could not understand its full significance?
Or because she belonged, like a certain other sinful woman,
to the category of those to whom much is forgiven because
they have loved much? We simply do not know. As St Paul
was to say, "The ways of God are mysterious".

CHAPTER VII

THE GOOD EARTH OF GALILEE

Jesus had had a definite reason for not staying in Judaea after the Passover of the year 28: his elder forerunner, John the Baptist, the man who had opened the way for him, had just been arrested and thrown into prison. This had happened simply because John had been faithful to his vocation as a prophet, because, like his predecessors in biblical times, he had reminded one of the great of his duty to observe the law of God.

In the domain left him by the Romans, Antipas, son of Herod the Great, kept a king's establishment and led a life of feasting. On the shores of the Lake of Genesareth he built a capital which he called Tiberias to flatter the reigning emperor. Antipas was a pleasure-seeker with little character. He had fallen in love with his sister-in-law Herodias, granddaughter of Herod the Great and the Hasmonaean princess Mariamna. Herodias was a fearsome person for whom this liaison marked a step forward in her career, since she did not consider that her old husband Herod Philip was capable of going very far.

When Herod Antipas' wife, an Arab princess from the kingdom of the Nabatheans, learnt about her husband's liaison, she returned to her father in Petra. Herodias took advantage of this to divorce Philip and wed her lover. In the eyes of the Law this was a scandal (Leviticus 18. 26; 20. 21).

John the Baptist told the tetrarch so plainly: "It is not permissible to marry thy brother's wife!" Herod Antipas might have resigned himself to letting the shaggy prophet shout, but according to the historian Josephus John's preaching was beginning to cause a stir in the little kingdom. Moreover, a woman like Herodias was not disposed to pardon the insult. So the Baptist was apprehended and taken off to a fortress in Moab, Macherus, which lay above the Dead Sea and was a Jewish outpost for keeping a watch on the Bedouins of the desert. He was thrown into a dungeon and was to speak no more (Matt. 14. 1–12; Mark 6. 17; Luke 8. 10).

Jesus now started on his ministry. His public life began at this precise moment. Back in his own province of Galilee, he spoke and was active before the crowds; instead of restricting hints about his character and message to a few disciples or people he met by chance, he showed himself forth publicly.

This period in Jesus' life, the essential period, cannot easily be reduced to a single, consecutive narrative. Since events at the beginning of his mission—baptism, retreat into the desert, meeting with Nicodemus—are reported only by St John, it is naturally the chronology of the Fourth Gospel which serves as a guiding thread in these early days. Henceforth, to establish the order of events we have to put the four gospels alongside each other and complete each of them by referring to the others. Like all ancient writers, their authors did not feel the need, which modern historians regard as elementary, to date events carefully and to relate them in the order in which they occurred. Thus indications of dates are extremely rare, except for the famous passage quoted earlier: "It was in the fifteenth year of the emperor Tiberius' reign. . . ." (Luke 3. 1, 2). For example, many journeys of Jesus are mentioned in the gospels, but no one says precisely how long each of them lasted.

To put together a connected narrative, and even to gain some idea of the total duration of Christ's mission, we have to note details and draw conclusions from them. For example, if three Passover feasts at which Jesus was present are mentioned, it may be deduced that his public life lasted more than two years. Minor references to "the green grass", to the harvests or to storms allow us to fix certain events in relation to the seasons. All this is no easy matter, especially as the Synoptics and St John are not always in agreement. That is why the debate about the length of Jesus' mission and the order of events, which was opened in the early days of the Church, is not yet closed.

The most likely and most generally accepted hypothesis can be formulated in this way. Jesus was baptized in January of the year 28, went up to Jerusalem in March for the Passover and probably began his public mission in Galilee towards the middle of May after learning of the arrest of John the Baptist. He stayed in his own province for about eighteen months, even celebrating the Passover of 29 there (the miracle of the multiplication of the loaves would fit in here) and only going up to Jerusalem later, perhaps for Pentecost. Episodes such as the calming of the storm and the Transfiguration could easily be situated in one or other of the seasons, the first in December when the north wind blows down on the Lake from Hermon, the second in August, in the dazzling sun. In the autumn of the year 29 Jesus went to Judaea, where he spent the winter of 30, and died at Jerusalem at the beginning of April.

Thus it was in Galilee, the little country of his youth, that Jesus began his public mission, amid a population which he had known since he was a child. It has often been said that there is a sort of symbolic correspondence between the two parts of Christ's mission and the regions in which they took place. The rugged, austere Judaea is the land of sacrificial revelations, of the sacrament which was to commemorate the death of the living God, of the drama by which this death was accomplished; Galilee, on the other hand, after the "charming miracle" of Cana, is the scene of wonderfully human miracles, such as the multiplication of the loaves, of the most moving meetings and of the consoling words of the Beatitudes.

Galilee is a small country, but a beautiful, varied and friendly one. Its red earth is fertile, "so fertile", says Josephus, "that it invites the least energetic to till the soil". Water is not wanting, whether it falls from the sky or comes down from the springs of Hermon. Thus all the Mediterranean crops flourish there—corn, barley, olives, vines, vegetables and fruit. In addition, the complex contours provide plenty of fine panoramas and views of blue hills dotted with the black flames of cypresses. The final touch is provided by the Lake of Genesareth; its clear waters are twelve miles long and six miles wide, and its shores are pleasantly lined with villages and townships.

The people of this fortunate region resembled their land in character; they were healthy, happy, simple and true. At Jerusalem, there was a tendency to look down on Galileans; their thick accent and rustic manner gave rise to laughter. But fair-minded witnesses acknowledged their great virtues: love of work, enthusiasm and loyalty. "In Galilee", said the rabbis, "honour counts for more than money." After all, Christ's first disciples were all Galileans.

When we think of the Gospel being preached for the first time, we tend to visualize it happening either on the shores of the Lake of Genesareth, with Jesus standing in a boat and addressing a crowd gathered on the shore, or else on a hill. But in fact this was to come a little later. Jesus' first sermons were preached in a quite different setting, the one in which any loyal Jew would have chosen to expound his religious views, the place where the Jews met, the synagogue.

The detail is worth stressing, for it shows Jesus deliberately acting in accordance with the tradition of Israel, seeking, as he was to say later, not to break with the Law but to fulfil it. St Luke lays emphasis on this preaching in synagogues; as the disciple of St Paul, a converted Pharisee, he fully appreciated its significance. He also makes it clear that Jesus was immediately successful in this sphere, for he says that "his praise was on all men's lips" (Luke 4. 15). At Cana, then, at Nazareth and at Capharnaum on the shore of the lake—where the ruins of the synagogue built by Antipas have been found—Jesus spoke in accordance with traditional practice.

The big synagogue ceremony took place on a Saturday, the Sabbath day. It began with prayers: standing with their faces turned towards Jerusalem, the congregation recited first the *Shema*, "Hear, O Israel, our God is one God", and the *Shemoneh Esreh*, the "eighteen benedictions". Then a scroll of the Law, that containing the Pentateuch, was taken out of the Ark and one of those present read one of 153 sections. A whole liturgy of readings and prayers followed, concluded by the "final lesson", which was awaited with curiosity. One of the faithful—anyone over the age of thirteen could seek this honour—read one, two or three verses from one of the prophetical books of the Bible and gave a free commentary on them. The custom followed by many Christian preachers of beginning their conference or sermon with a quotation from the Gospel is no different. This was called "acting as *maftir*".

During the early days of his mission in Galilee Jesus preached a sermon of this sort several times (cf. Mark 1. 21; Luke 4. 16–21). The biblical texts which he selected were certainly not chosen by accident. He was often heard to say that the appointed time had come and that the Kingdom of God was at hand (Mark 1. 15). According to St Luke, on one occasion he even went further towards indicating that he was the Messias by commenting on the passage in Isaias (61. 1): "The Lord has anointed me, on me his spirit has fallen; he has sent me to bring good news to men. . . ." But no one at that time understood who was denoted by these words.

It was not only by his words that Jesus began to draw attention to himself. A mysterious aura soon began to form round his person. His supernatural gifts could not pass unnoticed and the miracle at Cana had certainly not remained unknown.

A nobleman came to Jesus on the road leading down to Capharnaum; his son was lying sick there and he had come to ask Jesus to come down and heal the boy, for he was at the point of death. Jesus pointed out very clearly the nobleman's lack of faith: "You must see signs and miracles happen," he told him, "or you will not believe." If it is acknowledged that Jesus has the power of healing is there any need for him to go in person to the dying boy in order to cure him? But the nobleman repeated his request: "Sir, come down before my child dies." "Go back home," Jesus told him, "thy son is to live!" Galloping home, the officer meets a servant sent to meet him with the news that his son has been suddenly cured, at the precise moment when Jesus spoke to him (John 4. 48–54).

Sickness was thus conquered by a word from Jesus, and not sickness alone; more formidable powers were at his mercy. One day when he was speaking in a synagogue at Capharnaum a terrible noise broke out; a man rolled on the ground shrieking. It is well known that phenomena of this kind sometimes occur during religious services in monasteries; it is as if the evil Spirit sought to take revenge for the faith of those praying. In St Luke (4. 33–7) and St Mark (1. 23–8), the scene is a striking one. Jesus approaches the man possessed, commands the unclean spirit to leave him and in a few minutes order is restored.

We shall meet many other episodes of this kind. It seems that Jesus' thaumaturgic and supernatural powers very quickly became known in the whole region and that people came from all sides to beg him to use them on behalf of this or that unfortunate case. If he entered the house of a friend, that of Simon, for example, whom he met at the ford over the Jordan and surnamed "Peter", the latter immediately whispered to him, like a sort of challenge, that his mother-in-law was in very bad health and that he was counting on Jesus to heal her. If he rested in the evening on the shore of the lake, there were soon crowds of people with bandy legs, cripples and unbalanced persons round him, besieging him, begging him to help them. This enthusiasm must have sometimes worried him. What were these crowds going to do? Was it not possible that they would lay hold of him, proclaim him their leader—their earthly leader, of course, their king—and force him to take part with them in one of those absurd attempts at rebellion of which there had already been a number, and whose only result was to provoke severe repressive measures by the Romans?

At times like these, the Gospel tells us, Jesus would disappear. He would hide in some remote valley and spend the night alone, under the Father's eyes, as if to base his action all the more firmly on contemplation. This constant recourse to prayer is not the least important clue to the way in which Jesus understood his mission; it is as if, in these conversations with God, the Son of Man received from the divine power directives and impulses which guided his action on earth. It is the same for every believer; prayer alone illumines his path.

However, Jesus' success was bound to provoke reactions and to arouse suspicions. In this Jewish community, where everything to do with religion was the object of minute and zealous attention, it would have been inconceivable for a man to produce such spectacular manifestations, to set in motion supernatural forces, without immediately alerting the guardians of strict orthodoxy and the established order—the two were synonymous—namely the Scribes, the doctors of the Law, the leaders of the Jewish religious community, especially those of them who belonged to the rigorists, the Pharisees. The Pharisees had sympathizers everywhere, including Galilee; they constituted a sort of Holy League or Freemasonry throughout the country. Ostentatiously boasting of complete submission to the Torah, multiplying regulations, even on points of detail, so as to ensure fidelity to the traditional observances, they were certainly not all hypocrites, as the meaning which the word "pharisee" has acquired today might suggest; many of them were perfectly sincere people who wished God's will to be done—in their own way. But between their religion, with its legalism and formalism, and that of Christ, which was inspired by the great wind of the Spirit, conflict was inevitable.

Very early on in the young Galilean prophet's ministry they must have been on the alert, spying on him and ready to find fault. Indeed, they may have been entrusted by the political authorities with the task of keeping watch on him, for St Mark reports that Herod Antipas was disturbed by the activities of Jesus (Mark 6. 14).

CHAPTER VIII

FISHERS OF MEN

Jesus considered that he would have to have assistants in the huge task which he was undertaking, disciples specially chosen to collaborate with him. There were certainly men like this round John the Baptist; we are told that some of them came to see Jesus and to question him in the name of the imprisoned prophet. But the "general staff" set up by Christ was to assume a very special character, a character which was to have a decisive effect on the organism born of Christ, the Church.

At the ford over the Jordan a few men—five or six—Galileans like himself, had met Jesus and "followed him". They had travelled with him when he had returned to his own province; one or two of them had even witnessed the miracle at Cana; but none of them had yet taken the decision to leave everything and put himself completely at Jesus' disposal. These men were fishermen from the Lake of Genesareth; when he came to speak in this district Jesus met them —Simon Peter, for example—again, as we have just seen. And this was the moment of choice for them.

St Luke tells us, in one of the most beautiful passages in his gospel, of the circumstances in which several of them made the choice, circumstances which have a rich symbolic value. Jesus had just spoken to the people of the little fishing villages which form a white necklace round the lake. No doubt he had spent the night in the open air; in May, nights in the neighbourhood of the lake are exquisite. It was morning; a boat loomed out of the light mist, a good, solid boat capable of holding a dozen men. One of the oarsmen jumped out on to the shore and came up to Jesus. He seemed tired, and so did his comrades. It was Simon, Simon "the Rock". It had been a bad night; they had caught no fish. There was nothing in the *mehatten,* the vertical nets which are drawn up at dawn; and the *chabakah,* the cast-net, had been cast a score of times and brought in nothing. "Go back," said Jesus, "stand out into the deep water, and let down your net for a catch." The command seemed so absurd that for a moment Simon hesitated; but so absolute was his confidence in Jesus that he obeyed. The result was the "miraculous draught"; the nets were so heavy that they could hardly be pulled out of the water. Even more wonderful was the swift conclusion which the beneficiaries of the miracle drew from it: they immediately abandoned their nets and placed themselves under the orders of the Master. And Christ gave them the premonitory order, "Henceforth you shall be fishers of men".

Jesus' mysterious ability to win over a human being with one word, one look, was to succeed several times—twelve, to be exact—in snatching a man from his normal life and launching him into the great adventure of serving God. No one could evade the call, not even men apparently far from a spiritual vocation, such as Levi the publican, that is, an employee of the treasury or the customs, who was torn from his custom-house table by one phrase from Jesus, an imperious "follow me", to become the future evangelist, St Matthew (Matt. 9. 9; Mark 2. 14; Luke 5. 27).

There can be no doubt that these choices of Jesus were dictated by precise intentions and a clearly defined plan. A team of twelve men was formed. The number was important in itself, so important that when, after Christ's Passion, one of the twelve had disappeared, hasty steps were taken to replace him by Matthias. Jesus was to make this promise to his apostles: "You also shall sit there on twelve thrones, and shall be judges over the twelve tribes of Israel" (Matt. 19. 28). In Jewish symbolism, to speak of the "twelve tribes" was to allude to humanity as a whole. At the very moment when they were called these men were invested with a universal vocation.

It was a big rôle for such small men, "simple men, without learning", as they are described in Acts (4. 13), the very book which recounts the startling deeds performed by several of them. They all belonged to the same social class. They were neither poor nor rich; they were craftsmen earning an honest living, men whose fortune lay in their boats and nets. There was no intellectual among them, in the sense attached to the word in the Israel of that time; that is, there was no specialist in the Scriptures, no rabbi among them. Christ's power must have been great indeed to make these men participants in the great adventure. So true is it that, for the service of God, high qualities of intellect count less than those of the heart and the soul: will-power, loyalty, courage. The Galileans were well endowed with these.

What part did Jesus intend the Twelve to play? He meant them to be his envoys. The envoy, the *shaluhah*—in Greek *apostolos,* hence "apostle"—was, in Israelite usage, more than a messenger. He was entrusted with a mission, a man closely associated with the thought and work of the Master. We shall find the Apostles carrying out for Christ functions which we should describe as administrative, those assumed by the immediate collaborators of a political leader or a great missionary. If he plans a journey, it is they who go on ahead to find accommodation and to study the conditions in which he will be able to address the people. If he is speaking to a crowd, it is the Apostles who keep order, see that those present sit down, and sometimes even look after the feeding arrangements. But they do more.

When the Master gives them the order they set off two by two (this habit of sending out missionaries in pairs was to be maintained in the Church). Their task is to speak, to bear witness to the news of which Jesus is the sign and the living expression. "They are given power over unclean spirits. They can heal the sick, cleanse lepers, drive away devils and even raise the dead"; they are thus fully empowered representatives of the Son of God.

In order to carry out such enterprises successfully, they had to submit to certain demands and to receive a training from their Master. First of all, to follow him they had to abandon everything: family, trade, homeland. And when he made them his envoys, Jesus said to them: "Take neither gold nor silver, nor money in your purses. No change of clothing or of shoes!" They were in the service of a Master who taught contempt for earthly possessions and was himself the poorest of the poor. Above all, they had to be witnesses to what was to be the supreme lesson in their Master's teaching, that love, divine charity, comes before anything else.

In fact, these Apostles to whom, at his death, Jesus entrusted the fate of his work and of his community were very much as one sees them in the Gospels and subsequently in Acts. Most of them were clearly typed; they ranged from Simon Peter, the eldest, enthusiastic and devoted, prompt to speak and act, capable of sudden failures, but so straightforward, to the young and sensitive John, the Benjamin of the group, an adolescent for whom Jesus showed a particular love, even to the point of letting him lay his head on his breast. In between these two came James the Less, so pious that his knees became quite horny from kneeling, and Thomas, who owes his fame to his critical spirit. There was one misfit in this gallery of saints, Judas Iscariot, probably a Judaean, the mystery of whose life 2,000 years of exegesis have failed to elucidate. When Jesus, in his never-failing foreknowledge, chose Judas, he knew that one day he would be the human instrument of the fate decreed for him by providence.

Jesus did not confine himself to laying definite obligations on his envoys and giving them an austere training. He also endowed them with exceptional graces, as if by leading them to note his omnipotence he wished to strengthen their faith still further. Already those who had witnessed the miracle of the wedding at Cana had "believed in him"; their adhesion to Christ had been influenced by the event. They were to witness other sights at least as surprising.

Good examples are the two episodes of the storms. One night they were crossing the lake in the group's fishing boat in order to evangelize a different shore. Jesus had fallen asleep, tired out after a day's preaching. A violent wind arose, tossing the boat about severely. Terrified, the men woke their Master. He sat up, made a gesture, said a few words, and behold, the storm fell and the water grew calm (Luke 8. 22–5; Mark 4. 35–41; Matt. 8. 23–7). Another time, again at night, they were alone on the lake. A fresh wind drove them away from the shore; the oars were ineffective. They began to grow worried. If only the Master were there! Then suddenly there was this form gliding over the water. "Lord," exclaimed Peter, "if it is thyself, bid me come to thee over the water." And Jesus' hand prevented him from sinking in the waters which began to engulf him (Matt. 14. 23–33; Mark 6. 45, 46; John 6. 16–21).

The most extraordinary manifestation which it was granted to the Apostles to witness—an expressly messianic manifestation—fell to the lot of Peter, James and John. They had accompanied him to the top of a mountain—possibly Tabor or Hermon—when suddenly it seemed to them that his appearance, indeed his whole nature was changing. His whole being was made of light; even the sun was not more dazzling. Two mysterious presences flanked him on either side; they realized that these were Moses and the prophet Elias. And, as at the time of Jesus' baptism, a celestial voice resounded from a cloud, saying: "This is my beloved Son, in whom I am well pleased—to him, then, listen" (Matt. 17. 1–9; Mark 9. 1–12; Luke 9. 23–36). After such revelations, these men could hardly help being completely devoted to Jesus.

There is one point about this team picked by Christ to help him when he was alive and to continue his work when he was dead which is worth particular emphasis, namely, the hier-archical character of its organization. The great philosophers of antiquity, the Stoics for example, had disciples around them, but they were merely individuals; they did not form an entity. Christ's community, on the other hand, presents, very soon after its inception, a clearly marked organic and hier-archical character. The Twelve are expressly designated as the leaders of the faithful as a whole. Later on Jesus was to put alongside them the "Seventy-two", secondary apostles responsible for helping the Twelve in their tasks. And at the top of the whole organization he placed a leader or head.

It is quite possible that this system finds a parallel in that of the Essenes. Each Essene community was directed by a chief, the *Mebagger,* assisted by a council or chapter of twelve, which helped him to administer the monastery and considered cases of failure to keep the Rule. At the top, a supreme chief, the Teacher of Righteousness, had authority over all the members of the sect. We shall find a rather similar arrange-ment in the Church.

Who, then, was the leader of the little band of Apostles? As far as we can see, one of them did occupy a predominant posi-tion. When the first Apostles were called his figure stood out from the others. On the occasion of the miraculous draught, he alone had spoken; "Lord," he had stammered, "depart from me for I am only a sinful man", which was as good as saying that in Jesus he recognized much more than a man, the representative of the divine power, him of whom it would be said that he sounds hearts and minds. It was this same Apostle too who, on the night of the storm, had ventured to walk over the waters to meet the Master. He had also been one of the three privileged disciples before whose eyes Jesus had been transfigured, and on this occasion too he had spoken, daring to address God. This man so obviously marked out was none other than Simon, the Galilean fishing-boat captain, whom at their very first meeting Jesus had called to an exceptional destiny by changing his name. What we have already learnt about him and his character certainly shows that he had the ability to assume a wider command than that of half a dozen fishing nets and the men who hauled them in.

One day when Jesus was talking to his disciples during a halt by the roadside he asked them, half playfully: "What do people say about me? Who do they say I am?" "Some", replied the disciples, "assert that you are John the Baptist, others say that you are Elias, and others again that you are Jeremias or one of the prophets." "And what about yourselves," Jesus continued, "Who do you say that I am?" At that point Simon intervened quickly to say, "Thou art the Christ, the Son of the living God." His words had the character of an act of faith. At that time the Transfiguration had not yet taken place and Jesus had never expressly told his followers that he was the Messias.

Jesus looked at Simon as he had earlier on, not far from the ford, and said: "A good reply, Simon, and one that you can be happy to have given, for it was not flesh and blood but the Holy Spirit himself that dictated it to you." Then, employing once again the mysterious play on words which he had used when he changed his name from Simon to Peter, he went on to say: "And I tell thee this in my turn, that thou art Peter, and it is upon this rock that I will build my church; and the gates of hell shall not prevail against it. I will give to thee the keys of the kingdom of heaven; and whatever thou shalt bind on earth shall be bound in heaven; and whatever thou shalt loose on earth shall be loosed in heaven" (Matt. 16. 13–20; incomplete in the other two Synoptics).

The formulas used by Jesus had a meaning which a pious Jew, brought up in close touch with Scripture, was bound to understand. To hold the power of the keys, to be stronger than the gates of *Sheol*, were prerogatives of the Messias, and the comparison with the cornerstone or foundation stone was a classical one. This very important scene took place near the sources of the Jordan, in the region of forests and springs round the unshakable rocks of Hermon. Simon was to be truly the Rock and on this Rock the Church was to be built. It was the beginning of twenty centuries of Catholicism.

CHAPTER IX

JESUS SPEAKS

Surrounded by those whom he had chosen as his cooperators, Jesus continued and extended his mission in Galilee. Soon the setting of the synagogue probably seemed too narrow for his purpose; too narrow physically because these "houses of prayer" were never very big, nothing like so big as our churches, and too narrow spiritually because of the obligation on anyone who preached in them to stick closely to the verses from the Bible which he had quoted. So he abandoned the synagogues to teach bigger and bigger audiences; for St Mark soon shows him pressed and pursued by crowds, forced to jump into a boat and cross the lake when he was tired and wanted solitude. The only possible places to hold meetings were obviously the public squares in the towns or the open country, where so many prophets had spoken in days gone by and John the Baptist quite recently.

Jesus seems to have had two favourite spots for collecting his disciples. The first was the shore of the Sea of Galilee, or to be precise, one of its softly curving bays, with their heavenly sweetness, fringed with fine sand or backed by banks crowned with oleanders, which still inevitably suggest the charm of those days when the Gospel was first preached. The crowd would mass on the shore; the speaker would climb into a boat and move out about a dozen yards from the land. His voice carried well over the water. The second site was a peaceful spot in the hills, a little valley forming a natural amphitheatre, a grassy slope with a rock set in the ground half-way up it and forming a rostrum.

Just such a spot was the setting, during the Galilean period, probably towards the end of June in the year 28, of Christ's most famous and most admirable piece of teaching; the "Sermon on the Mount", also known as "the Beatitudes", because of the exclamations with which it begins, "Blessed are those. . . ." It was already hot in the valley at this time of year; Jesus "went up on to the mountainside", that of Tabgah perhaps, eight miles from Tiberias and two miles from Capharnaum, or the rather more remote plateau with two peaks known as Karn Hattin, where, in 1187, Saladin settled accounts decisively with the army of the Frankish kingdom of Jerusalem. Arriving at the spot which he had marked out, Jesus stopped; the crowd gathered round him and sat down on the ground. He began to speak, and what he said forms a complete but spontaneous summary, not in the least didactic, of what he was to tell men all through his public mission. When one reads St Matthew, who describes the scene in detail (Matt. 5, 6, 7), one really feels that one is on a peak.

Addressing crowds clearly demands qualities quite different from those needed to give a commentary on Scripture. There can be no doubt that Jesus possessed these qualities. His success is only explicable as the inevitable consequence of great oratorical gifts. In Israel, as in the rest of the East, considerable importance was attached to the spoken word. Literature, in the sense which we give to the term, was a branch of oratory; the books of the Bible had been spoken aloud before being written down, and the Koran of Mohammed was in fact dictated. All the illustrious leaders of ancient Israel, such as David and Solomon, had been masters of the spoken word. When Yahweh chose Moses to lead his people, Moses tried to evade the heavy task by arguing that he was a bad speaker (Exod. 4. 10). Jesus could certainly not have pleaded this excuse for not undertaking his mission.

Jewish oratory was very different from modern Western eloquence. The clear arrangement of ideas, logical demonstration, rational sequence of sentences, in fact all the things we have learnt from Cicero were quite alien to it. The object was not so much to convince the audience by logic as to exert a direct and perceptible effect on it which, by establishing contact between the speaker and the listener, inclined the latter to let himself be persuaded. To attain this result the Israelite orator often had recourse to a rhythmic style, full of deliberate repetitions, hesitations, calculated antitheses, alliterations, even puns. Another way of capturing an audience's attention was to insert plenty of explicit or implicit references, or at any rate allusions, to the Scriptures, on which a Jew was brought up from his most tender years; everyone would recognize the passage which the speaker had in mind. These techniques gave Jewish oratory an extraordinary sonority and power of suggestion. We find all this in the eloquence of Jesus.

All this and more, for even through two translations—from Aramaic into Greek, and from Greek into a modern language—Jesus' words retain a quite unparalleled force and originality. The phrases that sprang from his lips possess, as Renan pointed out, "a sort of brilliance that is both gentle and terrible, a divine force, so to speak, which detaches them from their context and makes them easily recognizable". We understand what Renan meant when we read sentences like "let the dead bury their dead" or "the first shall be last". A master of the spoken word by Israelite standards, Jesus has retained this mastery right down the centuries and in every conceivable ethnic and linguistic setting. The reason for this is that, as St John puts it in a play on words which hints at the greatest of all mysteries, he was himself the *Logos*, the Word of God.

Those who followed Jesus closely—his disciples in particular—could not fail to notice that his mode of expression was not always the same and that, in the second part of the

Galilean period, it changed completely. In general, and especially at the start, his teaching was direct, simple and accessible to everyone. The short phrases he used were clear, categorical and striking: "Let thy speech be yea, yea or nay, nay." It was impossible for anyone to mistake the meaning of commands such as "Love thy neighbour as thyself"; "no one can serve God and Mammon"; "If thou fastest, anoint thy head". Two thousand years have not blunted the edge of these aphorisms or weakened their power to warn.

Yet this imperious simplicity was not always the dominant note in Jesus' oratory. Sometimes the thread of the discourse would be clothed in a sort of story or brief fable with a moral or spiritual lesson. These little stories must have been strung out at intervals along the Master's discourses—although the Synoptics group the principal ones together—playing, among others, the part of the anecdote in the work of a lecturer who knows his job, that of retaining the audience's attention. These little stories are called "parables", from the Greek word meaning "comparison".

As a matter of fact, in the Israel of that period, the difference between an exposition of doctrine and the apologues which found a natural place in it as illustrations was less marked than it would be today. The Hebrew word *mashal*, which is translated by the Greek "parabola", is in fact much wider in scope than the latter. The *mashal* formed an integral part of the Hebrew tongue, which is concise, vivid, excellent at expressing the concrete, but clumsy when it comes to defining abstractions and metaphysical notions; it gets out of the difficulty by using images, symbols and comparisons, a device completely in line with Israelite psychology, which is extremely intuitive, sees at once the topical, realistic, familiar side of a thing, and excels at drawing a lesson from it. The *mashal* was just that; a way of looking at a piece of behaviour or a situation so as to draw a moral from it. A saying like "Physician, heal thyself" was a *mashal*. It simply happened that observed facts lent themselves to anecdote and that the lessons to be drawn from them were not always perfectly obvious. The parables in the gospels are excellent pieces of literature, in which Renan was right to see "something analogous to Greek sculpture, where the ideal can be touched and loved". Parables were to be heard on Christ's lips right up to the last days of his life. Of the twenty or so which occur in the synoptic gospels—St John does not quote one—half at least are so famous that the substance of them has become part of Western civilization. We have only to think of the parables of the Sower, the Good Seed and the Tares, the Good Samaritan, the Wise and Foolish Virgins, or the Prodigal Son, to realize that Western art would not be what it is if these little stories had never existed.

However, it must be acknowledged that they do not all lead to easily definable conclusions. The parable of the Unjust Steward, who is praised for his skill, which to human eyes looks extraordinarily like roguery, and that of the lilies of the fields, which seems to recommend complete idleness, have always taxed preachers' ingenuity. It is also quite comprehensible that the disciples should have asked Jesus why he had recourse to these stories which were so difficult to understand. Christ's reply (Matt. 13. 10–17) was hardly less disconcerting; he said that it was so that everyone should not understand!

Yet that was the truth. If Jesus' message was to spread, it had to obey the economy of revelation. Its staggering novelty would have shocked people even more than it actually did if it had all been expressed quite clearly. The morality of the parables is often so paradoxical that it could almost be described as scandalous; think, for example, of the Prodigal Son or the workman who started at the eleventh hour. In principle, Christ's message was directed against a formalistic morality, against a banal religion of debit and credit. Resistance in the name of sound principles and the established order was soon to be vigorous. One can understand that Jesus did not wish to make his boldest and strongest points clear right from the outset.

So what Jesus gave the crowds who gathered to listen to him was a new message. Of what did it consist? We can gain a clear idea of its main lines by reading the Sermon on the Mount as reported by St Matthew (5, 6, 7), who is supplemented on a few points by St Luke (6). The passage is so rich in content and so perfect in form that it has been described as containing "the quintessence of the Gospel". The other parts of Jesus' teaching connect up with it or carry it further.

Christ is speaking to all believers who await "the Kingdom of Heaven", that kingdom whose precise nature several parables try to explain. It is an ineffable reality "within us"; each of us carries in him the tiny seed of it like a grain of mustard seed. This tiny seed can grow enormously, just as the mustard seed becomes a tree; it is the supreme good to which all are invited if they wish, like guests invited to a marriage feast.

What must we do to possess this kingdom? In a sense, just one thing: make a choice. We must opt for God, for the Spirit, for what does not pass away; not, as most men do, for what does pass away, for the world. "Real treasure is in heaven." This choice of God is an act of love; the believer will love God with all his heart, with all his mind and with all his strength, he will love him above all things. But this love has, as it were, another facet, love of men; "love thy neighbour as thyself" is the second commandment and it is identical with the first. Several rabbis of Israel had already said that, but it would certainly have been rash to think that the whole people made it a maxim of its conduct.

To these two great principles was added another rather more subtle one which marked a step forward. This was the appeal for a truly inward religion, a religion based not on submission to rituals or precepts, but on honesty of purpose and purity of intention. It was not only murder that was wrong but mere anger, the inward upsurge of violence which, even if it does not result in any action, urges us to injure others. It was no longer only adultery which was reproved, but the lecherous glance at an attractive woman. Blasphemy, the insult to God's name, was certainly detestable, but so was the false protestation which makes it possible to perform a wicked deed under the cover of a good conscience. God judges us by what is in our hearts; judge not if you do not wish to be judged.

All this was quite new, but Jesus went further still. To possess the kingdom it was not enough to have a pure heart and an honest will; one had to allow a complete reversal of situations and intentions. This was proclaimed by the famous apostrophes of the Beatitudes. Blessed are the patient, blessed are the merciful, blessed are the pure in heart, blessed are the peacemakers! This too could be accepted quite easily; since Moses' time it had been known that God rewarded moral virtues. But according to Christ the kingdom was promised just as much, or more, to the unfortunate, the hungry, the poor, the persecuted, that is, those whom the world pities and sometimes helps a bit, but whom it has never agreed to regard as happy.

"The Kingdom is the world upside down", said a Jewish rabbi in a phrase recorded in the Talmud. That was certainly the logical conclusion of Jesus' teaching. "You have heard that it was said, An eye for an eye and a tooth for a tooth. But I tell you, Love your enemies!" What a curious morality this was, which upset all the principles of the social order. Offer the left cheek if you have received a blow on the right one! It was as inadmissible as paying the workman who started at the eleventh hour as much as those who had worked hard all day, or as doing for the badly behaved son, on the pretext that he was coming home, what one had never done for his sensible and loyal elder brother. It is always difficult to accept that divine grace does not obey the distributive principles of human justice.

It goes without saying that teaching of this sort was the exact opposite of the formalism and legalism which have been honoured in every age with the name of religion. The good devotees of the Torah were not sorry that it should be known that they prayed well, fasted according to the rules or even a little more, and gave alms when they were due. But Jesus asked a good deal more of them; he asked them to do all this in secret—"If thou fastest, anoint thy head"—so that only God should see these meritorious actions; only then would they have any merit.

This was the way in which Jesus talked to those whom he called to be "the salt of the earth", the "light of the world", that is, the bearers of these new truths. He had no illusions about the resistance he would meet in preaching this message; he told his disciples that they would be insulted and persecuted as the prophets had been. He even knew from what quarter this resistance would come; from those for whom religion was primarily a matter of form, practice and conformity. He proclaimed, it is true, that he had not come "to set aside the Law" (Matt. 5. 17) and that "not an iota of it would be changed"; but he also spoke of "perfecting" the Law. People were bound to be anxious about the precise meaning he attached to this word.

CHAPTER X

LOYALTY AND OPPOSITION

Nevertheless, as St Luke tells us, "his fame spread more and more" (Luke 5. 15), and St Mark adds that "they came in multitudes to listen to him and to be healed by him". Such is certainly the impression we derive from reading the accounts of this Galilean period, the impression of a success. In this happy land the good seed falls and seems to take root easily. The opposition has not yet crystallized sufficiently to interfere with the effect of Christ's radiant presence. It is a time of happiness and hope.

What confident faces were to be seen round Jesus in those days! There were not only the Apostles, the first disciples, who had left everything to follow him and lead a haphazard life, without hearth or home, dependent on people's generosity; there were not only those devoted women who, we can guess, followed him about, looking after the material things, but there were also the numerous, nameless people who spent hours watching for his arrival, then listening to him, people who followed him right out to the hills, forgetful of time and even omitting, as we shall see, to take any food with them. There was an upsurge of enthusiasm for the young Messias, a foretaste of the fervour which the sublime figure of Jesus was to arouse in men's hearts right down the centuries.

A number of individuals stand out from the throng because their faith in Jesus was rewarded immediately. All through the gospels we meet them: despairing invalids who turn their gaze on him, parents and friends trembling for the life of a dear one, sinners who have plumbed the depths of human misery and have no other recourse but him whom they recognize as the Master who can grant forgiveness. There is Jairus, the ruler of the synagogue, whose daughter is dying and who turns in his distress to the new prophet that has arisen in Israel. There is the woman with the issue of blood or haemorrhage; she does not dare to explain the painful condition to the Master, but sneaks up to him surreptitiously, convinced that if she can touch the hem of his cloak she will be cured; and she is. There is the paralytic who has himself let down to Jesus on ropes, through the roof, and the other man whom Christ puts back on his feet on a short visit to Jerusalem, at the pool of Bethsaida. One could say of all these what Jesus himself said to one of them, it was their faith that made them whole.

Two of these people of great faith are particularly famous and worthy of admiration. The first is the centurion of Capharnaum, the man whom the French soldier-author, Ernest Psichari, was to salute as a perfect example of all the military virtues. The servant of this junior officer is in danger of dying; the officer appeals to the healing prophet; but, overcome by scruples, he sends messengers to Jesus to say that there is no need for him to put himself out; let him simply give the order from a distance and the centurion is sure, as a soldier who knows how effective commands are, that the supernatural forces will obey. Jesus himself praises and sets up as a model this sublime confidence. Such a confident request was bound to be granted (Luke 7. 1–10; Matt. 8. 5–13).

The second person is a still more touching figure, indeed the most moving one in the whole Gospel after Mary, in whatever situation we meet her. I refer to the public sinner, the woman of Magdala, whom people point to with a grin; she is daring enough to insinuate herself into the room when Jesus is eating his meal with a respectable host simply to weep at his feet and to pour ointment on them. Jesus welcomes her with all his mercy (Luke 7. 36–50). It is a lovely scene and one that awakens so many echoes in everyone's heart that St Gregory the Great said of it: "When I contemplate it, I want to weep silently."

The extent of the stir caused by Jesus' mission was revealed in a surprising way. John the Baptist had now been imprisoned in some sinister dungeon in the fortress of Macherus for nearly a year and already seemed to be quite cut off from the world of the living, but in the East rumour, "the bird's wing", as it was called, paid no heed to the thickest walls or the strongest iron bars. The Precursor got wind of what was happening in Galilee, and may have wanted to find out if the man of whom so many wonderful things were told was the one on whom the Holy Spirit had settled before his own eyes, or else perhaps to have the messianic character of his mission confirmed. Anyway, emissaries from the Baptist appeared before Jesus.

"Are you he who is to come?" they asked him, "or are we to await another?" Jesus' reply was as clever as it was conclusive. To proclaim himself publicly as the Messias straightway was not part of his plan, so he replied in these words: "Go and tell John what you have seen and heard: the blind see, the lame walk, lepers are cleansed and the poor have the gospel preached to them!" To Jews soaked in the Scriptures, the allusion to verses 5–6 in Chapter 35 of Isaias was clear; it was in these precise words that the great prophet had described the messianic era. The messengers from the Baptist were able to go away again content (Luke 7. 18–23; Matt. 11. 2–6).

To these concrete proofs of his messianic nature Jesus could have added many others; the fact, for example, that the hungry were fed, for it was at this very period that he performed—on two occasions, so it seems—a truly astonishing miracle and one rich in symbolism.

The scene was Bethsaida-Julias, right at the north of the lake, near the point where the Jordan, still a mere stream, flows into it. Jesus had come to this fairly remote spot in the hope of gaining a little peace for prayer and rest, but the crowd had sensed this, as crowds always do, and it was there before he had even had a chance to find a resting-place. He was obliged to take up again the burden of teaching and healing. Time passed, and it was growing late; what were all these people to eat? They were far from their homes and had brought nothing with them. The disciples began to feel worried.

But Jesus gave his orders quite calmly. He told his disciples to make the people sit down in companies. The disciples knew how to arrange this: in fifties, hundreds and thousands, as at Essene gatherings. Then he told them to collect anything eatable they could find in the crowd. The result was derisory: five loaves of barley bread and two small salted fish. But Jesus did not seem to be disappointed; he blessed these miserable odds and ends, and called down on them the divine power of the Creator. Immediately there was a miracle which it is impossible to understand or even to describe: the loaves multiplied and filled the baskets in which they were hastily piled. The food was distributed and there was more than enough for everyone (Matt. 15. 29–39; Mark 6. 30–44; Luke 9. 10–17; John 6. 1–15).

Later on, this miracle was to be compared with a mystery in which bread again plays the central part. People remembered a discourse on the "bread of life" which Jesus gave a short time afterwards. This bread, multiplied to satisfy bodily hunger, was compared with another kind of food, itself infinitely multiplied, intended to nourish souls. Jesus himself seems to have suggested this comparison in advance, for on the very next day after the miracle, speaking to his audience, he said: "You gather round me because you were fed with loaves. But the true bread is not perishable food. It is not the manna that Moses gave you; it is the bread of Heaven."

It would have been pleasant if nothing had occurred to mar the splendour and happiness of this Galilean period and Jesus' whole mission had been completed amid peaceful enthusiasm, but he himself said on several occasions that Providence had ordained otherwise. The grace of God cannot be sown in sinful humanity without provoking resistance and opposition. There were hints of these right from the start of Jesus' ministry; at first they simply took the form of distrust, but they were soon to grow clearer and stronger.

Some of this opposition sprang from very human causes, as is shown by an incident which occurred at Nazareth. The reputation acquired by Jesus had reached his native village, and the good people of the district were quite proud of it. So when the young prophet was visiting his mother they gathered round him and tried to persuade him to show his fellow citizens the great things that he had done at Capharnaum and elsewhere. What they wanted was a miracle to order, to please his friends at Nazareth. But Jesus evaded the invitation; it was only too clear that people who expected a miracle from him had understood nothing. He refused, and made matters worse by telling those round him that the fact that they might be neighbours or relations gave them no particular right to enjoy a special grace and that they had only to open the Bible to see that many of the most moving miracles had been performed for the benefit of foreigners, of pagans. This kind of language has never pleased public opinion. There was disappointment, bad temper, anger; it was a miracle that, tugged and jostled, Jesus was not thrown from the top of a cliff towards which the crowd had pushed him (Luke 4. 22–30; Matt. 13. 54–8).

Hostility of this sort was only episodic; other kinds were more serious because they sprang from more permanent causes. St Mark (2, 3) and St. Luke (5, 6) relate a series of five incidents which occurred between Jesus and the Pharisees entrusted with the task of keeping a watch on him. They all point in the same direction. They show Jesus calmly opposing the formalism and narrow legalism of the Pharisees, although in the synagogue, as we have seen, he had always behaved as a faithful observer of the Jewish tradition. What he taught had nothing in common with the quibbles of the rabbis, with the pedantic scholasticism to which some people tried to reduce religion. St Paul's phrase, "The letter kills, it is the Spirit that gives life", sums up perfectly the attitude of Jesus in this fundamental dispute.

There can be no doubt that there were sufficient grounds for a conflict in this debate. Many of Jesus' words and actions must have touched the Pharisees to the quick. There was his habit of paying no attention to the strict and detailed rules drawn up by generations of rabbis to govern the Sabbath, the holy day of rest. He healed the sick on the Sabbath, he allowed his disciples to prepare a simple meal and even to work. "The Sabbath was made for man, not man for the Sabbath"; there was something sacrilegious in the formula. Fasting, another religious custom imposed by rigorous regulations, did not seem to be sacred either, according to what this disquieting innovator said. He also jeered at the tithe, the holy tithe which provided such a good living for the priests of Israel, by daring to assert that God did not measure a man's generosity by calculating the amount he gave in tithes. He seemed to defy normal notions of respectability by admitting among his followers the most impure and contemptible people, women of loose morals and publicans such as Levi, the exciseman whom he had made one of his Twelve Apostles. Jesus realized all this. He knew that the conflict between himself and those who stuck to the letter of the law was a mortal one. When he spoke of those "old bottles" in which new wine could not be put, the allusion was quite clear. As for the Pharisees, they understood the situation just as clearly.

If anyone had forgotten that it was dangerous to say certain things in the name of God, a dramatic incident occurred at this point to remind them. News of it was brought to Jesus, probably in March of the year 29: the Baptist had been put to death. John's disciples came, by his express command, to tell the prophet of Galilee what had happened.

Imprisoned in the depths of a Moabite fortress, the Forerunner cannot have constituted a very great danger. Left to himself, Herod Antipas would have probably taken no further action, keeping John in his sight but not committing himself about the future; the historian Josephus says that the tetrarch "liked a quiet life". But this was reckoning without the vindictive temper of Herodias, the woman whom he had illegally made his wife. The Hasmonaean blood which flowed in her veins was proud and passionate. John had treated her publicly as an adulteress and Herodias was not the woman to forgive an insult like this.

Hence the famous episode commemorated so often in literature, the theatre and painting. The royal caravan, returning from a visit to Babylon, halted at Macherus. There was a typically Eastern feast there, with interludes of music and dancing. The most seductive of the dancers was Salome, the daughter of Herodias. Already half-tipsy, the tetrarch completely lost his head as he watched this attractive young creature. "Ask for whatever you would like", he exclaimed. He was thinking no doubt of some jewel or a purse full of gold, but what was demanded of him came into a rather different category. "Ask for the Baptist's head!" whispered Herodias to her daughter. "He must grow and I must diminish", the Prophet had said. A woman's hatred was the instrument of this sacrificial vocation (Matt. 14. 1–12; Mark 6. 14–29; Luke 9. 7–9).

This event was the harbinger of another sacrifice. Every now and then in this peaceful Galilean period a sinister warning would ring out, like a dissonance shattering the harmony. On one occasion the warning came in connection with the Baptist himself. When Jesus was asked if it was possible that John was Elias returned to earth, he replied that the Forerunner had certainly been given the rôle assigned to Elias in Scripture, that of preparing the way for the messenger of the Lord, but, like John himself, the messenger would have to suffer and die (Mark 9. 10–13; Matt. 17. 9–13). On another occasion—it was after Peter's confession of faith and his designation as leader, "Thou art Peter, and on this rock. . . ."—Jesus added one or two details to this prophetic announcement, predicting that he would be put to death and also that he would rise again (Luke 9. 22; Mark 8. 31; Matt. 16. 21). On yet another occasion, just after the glorious scene of the Transfiguration, as if he wished to prevent the three witnesses of the theophany from mistaking its significance, Jesus repeated: "The Son of Man will be delivered into the hands of men; they will put him to death, and on the third day after his death he will rise again" (Mark 9. 30; Luke 9. 44; Matt. 17. 21).

Did the faithful disciples understand at that time what these words meant? The Gospel answers, "No, they could not understand his meaning". Indeed, they understood so little that Peter replied to one of these terrible predictions with the words, "Never, Lord, no such thing shall befall thee". The reply earned him a severe rebuke: "Back, Satan; thou art a stone in my path, for those thoughts of thine are man's, not God's." They certainly were man's thoughts. No doubt the disciples still hoped that the Master to whom they had given themselves was the powerful Messias dreamed of by Israel, who would restore his people to glory, and that they, his friends, would fare well as a result of his victory. For after all they were only men, and they were still far from fathoming the great mystery of the necessity for suffering, of redemption by blood.

CHAPTER XI

JESUS THE MAN

One would like to try to visualize this extraordinary man whose mere presence exercised a magnetic attraction on crowds, and who steadily developed his activities day by day, asserting himself with sovereign power, but a preliminary question arises: to what extent do the four gospels provide the material for a portrait of Jesus? The authors' aims were obviously quite different; these four simple men had no literary or psychological pretensions. As the witnesses of events which had completely transformed their lives, or as the disciples of masters who had witnessed them, their only purpose was to give an account of the "Good News" which they had received, without artifice and without any attempt at interpretation.

The astonishing thing is that from their four accounts, which differ on certain points—indeed, the fourth is quite different from the first three in intention and tone—a unique, unquestionably genuine figure does emerge and takes possession of the reader's imagination. This is enough in itself to dispose of the hypothesis of certain "independent critics" that Jesus was invented by the first Christians, fabricated out of biblical and legendary reminiscences—the "eschatological" Christ of Guignebert, or the "mythical" Christ of Couchoud. It is difficult to understand how four different minds could create the one same character out of material such as this, and achieve straighway the dream of every novelist, the creation of a true living being.

Nonetheless, the portrait of Jesus which can be constructed from the gospels is from many points of view disappointing, first of all because there are gaps in it which a modern writer would not have left, but especially—and this is much more far-reaching—because however closely we study this portrait we always end up with a number of elements which are incomprehensible. Every man has something about him that cannot be analysed, the secret that he carries within himself; how much more must this be true of the being whose human flesh and spirit harboured the most unfathomable of mysteries, the presence of God.

There is one realm, in any case, in which curiosity is quite pointless, since the evangelists did not have the slightest idea that they ought to give the reader any information on this particular point, namely the physical appearance of Jesus the man. Almost all ancient writers are unaware of possible interest in this point, unlike modern novelists and even historians, who take care to describe their principal characters' features, trying to relate them more or less to the psychology of the persons concerned. It is absurd to claim to be able to glean information about the physical appearance of Jesus from the gospel narratives; to infer, for example, from the scene in which the publican Zacchaeus climbs a tree so as to see him better that he was small in stature and lost in the crowd; or to assert that he was radiantly beautiful because Mary Magdalen recognized him straightway among the guests at a banquet.

Of course, holiness or genius does sometimes shine forth from the features of an exceptional person, and we have a deep-seated wish that this may have been so with Christ. Stronger than any reasoning is the faithful soul's love for him, which would like to think that the Divine Master, the Consoler, looked like a Christ by Van Eyck or El Greco. In fact, however, no one can answer the question, was Jesus handsome, tall, nobly built? The only valid opinions are those expressed by St Polycarp and St Augustine, one of whom says, "The physical appearance of Jesus is unknown to us", and the other, "We are quite unaware what his face was like."

All the traditions which have claimed to hand on to posterity information about the features and stature of Jesus are based on legends or tendentious interpretations of Scripture. A good example of them is the charming fable which sees in St Luke a talented artist who painted a portrait of Jesus at the request of the Virgin Mary. It is true that, of the four evangelists, the third is the one who seems to have been most concerned to portray Jesus, to bring him to life, but the portrait is a literary one. If we apply to Christ biblical phrases regarded as giving prophetic indications about the Messias, we end up with completely contradictory descriptions. For instance, if we follow verse 3 of Psalm 44, we can assert that he was "the fairest of the children of men"; if, on the other hand, we remember Isaias' famous words (53) about the suffering Messias, or the similar verses in Psalm 21, we shall visualize him as a sickly and pitiful being, destined in advance to suffer the blows of human wickedness. A number of more or less famous forgeries, such as the *Letter of Lentulus,* which achieved great popularity in the fourteenth century, have sprung from one current of tradition or the other.

One last problem arises. In the absence of any solid information in the Gospel, is the question of the physical appearance of Jesus settled by the existence of a piece of evidence which claims to provide an actual portrait of him, a sort of photographic likeness? Some people assert that it is. This piece of evidence is the cloth preserved in Turin cathedral and commonly known as the "Holy Shroud". According to those who claim that it is authentic, this is the actual winding-sheet in which Jesus was wrapped during the forty hours or so which he spent in the tomb. The image is certainly there, like a negative on a photographic plate; it is the life-size picture of a man bearing the wounds and stigmata which, according to the accounts in the gospels, one would expect to

see on a man crucified. When one takes a print of the negative, the face which appears is striking, almost superhuman;
"appallingly veracious", Claudel called it. It is the sort of
countenance that one could look at for ever. Unfortunately the
circumstances surrounding the Shroud are such that it is just
as difficult to accept it as authentic as it is to prove that it is
not.

When it comes to visualizing Jesus' behaviour, to seeing
how he lived, we are on much firmer ground. The gospels are
full of little details which we can connect with what we know
of Jewish life at that time. Jesus looks like one among others
in this little community of Galilean peasants, craftsmen and
fishermen from which he had sprung, amid which he had
lived for so many years, and where his activities began. He
looks, in fact, like an ordinary man.

We have already noted that his name was a common one;
there must have been many men called Jesus or Joshua, sons
of a Joseph and a Mary. He lived exactly as the people of his
native district did. Like them, he ate mainly bread, fish and
fruit; meat was kept for special occasions. However, he did
not refuse to eat a more elaborate meal from time to time
when he was invited by a friend, nor did he decline a few
glasses of the thick, dark wine which was always watered
before it was drunk. His clothes, too, were those that everyone
wore: the tunic or *chalouk* of wool or linen, hand-woven by
women, seamless if it was meant to be a good one, fringed at
the bottom with the hyacinth-blue ritual tassels, the *tsitsith,*
which the woman with the haemorrhage touched in order to be
healed; and the cloak or *talith,* a rough, sturdy garment for
all occasions, providing good protection against the icy winds
of winter and useful all the year round for sleeping in out of
doors.

The languages that Jesus spoke were also those in daily use.
First there was Aramaic, the Semitic dialect employed for
centuries more or less throughout the Levant; the Gospel
quotes a number of phrases in it, such as *Talitha cumi*

(Maiden, arise) and *Eloi, lama sabacthani* (Lord, why hast thou forsaken me?). Then there was Hebrew, which every Jew had to be capable at least of reading and translating, since it was the liturgical language, *la Leshon ha Kodeth*, the language of holiness; when he spoke in the synagogues, Jesus had proved that he could read the Scriptures. Finally, it is more than probable that Jesus spoke Greek, for at his trial he conversed with the Roman Pilate without an interpreter. From one end of the Empire to the other, almost everyone knew the popular Greek, or *koinê*, used for business and administration.

All this is important. In the life that we see him leading in the pages of the Gospel, Jesus behaves in an entirely human fashion. He was a true man, and the fact must be emphasized in view of certain heresies of the first few centuries which tried to maintain that his humanity was only a fiction, a sort of screen masking his divinity. The real situation was quite different. The phrase "Son of Man" which he liked to apply to himself, for an Israelite *ben Adam* or *bas nasha*, meant primarily "a man", even if it awoke strange messianic echoes, as we shall see. He was a man, the son of man, a "thinking reed", as Fr Grandmaison puts it, and so he appears throughout the Gospel. He was a man of sensibility, betraying human reactions and even passion. Not only do we see him showing hunger and thirst, and letting himself fall, tired out, on to the edge of a well or the bottom of a boat, but on several occasions he betrays human feelings and does not try in the least to preserve a transcendent serenity. He makes no secret of his affection for a young disciple, for a family with which he is friendly, or even chance acquaintances, such as the "rich young man". Before the tomb of his friend Lazarus, he who has the power to conquer death—and is going to prove it—does not restrain his emotion, his tears. Even anger is not unknown to him, tinged with scorn to reply to Herod Antipas, "the fox", bursting out in fury at the scandal of the squalid commerce being conducted openly in the Temple. There is a still more human moment when, in his agony, he bends under the blows of the terrible spiritual storm that has descended on him and admits his anguish. These are all aspects of Jesus the man, the true man that he was.

But there is more to it than this. It may be impossible to draw a physical portrait of Jesus, but the gospels yield a psychological portrait—or, at any rate, one that may be provisionally described as "psychological"—a portrait so alive and so complete that it would be impossible to wish for a more precise or evocative one, the portrait of a man whose temperament and character burn themselves into the reader's mind and leave an ineradicable impression on it.

Jesus was a remarkably well-balanced man. Well balanced physically, for a start; the man whom we see in action continuously for two and a half years, walking long distances in every weather, speaking to big audiences in the open air, withstanding the fatigue caused by the continual proximity of followers, the inquisitive and beggars, was obviously a solid, healthy man, as we should expect a countryman of thirty to be. He was also certainly well balanced mentally; one would be almost ashamed to make the point if self-styled critics had not spoken of "the madness of Jesus", and if psychiatrists had not visualized him as schizophrenic or paranoiac, although everything we know about him reveals a sense of reality and proportion which gives the lie to these absurd theories. We must be grateful to Renan for disposing of them so contemptuously: "The madman never succeeds. So far it has not been granted to a wandering mind to exert any serious effect on the progress of humanity."

To the unprejudiced reader of the gospels the personality of Jesus seems, on the contrary, perfectly coherent and solid, built up on an unshakable foundation. There is nothing in him of that almost unconscious artifice to be observed so often in human relations, which urges even the best men to convey a favourable picture of themselves. If he had been "an impostor", as was maintained in an impious book circulating at the court of Frederick II of Hohenstaufen, the excommunicated German emperor, it is quite obvious that he would have sought to set up an earthly kingdom.

He was sincere, but also firm. We never see him letting himself be driven by events or by requests to do things he does not want to do. He eludes the enthusiastic crowds when he considers it necessary, and he refuses to gratify his fellow-citizens of Nazareth with a miracle. He confronts resistance and opposition only at the moment which he has chosen himself. At his trial, the different ways in which he replies to the high priests, to Herod and to Pilate reveal an attitude which is quite the reverse of indifference to human prudence. Even in circumstances where he could well be "beside himself", for instance when he gives vent to his indignation with the traders in the Temple, one has the impression that his anger is intended and controlled, that it is inspired by love. The Apocalypse calls it "the vengeance of the Lamb" (6. 16). "His Spirit was subject to him," says the Gospel. If ever a man was master of himself, it was Jesus.

Based on this sound psychological foundation, the personality of the young Messias is an exceptionally harmonious one. Greatness and simplicity go hand in hand in it; and this is always a mark of the greatest distinction in a man. It presupposes "a sense of what is really important", as Fr Grandmaison rightly says, "a feeling for fine distinctions, a habitual self-possession and self-forgetfulness that no training can achieve and no talent can make up for". Its most striking characteristic is perhaps wisdom, a sort of sublime tranquillity in the face of events and other people which prevents its owner ever being deceived by appearances, which allows him to form a just opinion of men without ceasing to love them.

For that is the culminating point of this rich personality: an infinite power of welcome, a constant upsurge of love. Nothing repels him. The dominating force in him is "the heart", in the sense that Pascal gives this word when he makes it not only the seat of the emotions but also a means of knowing people and things. The hackneyed phrase "gentle Jesus" must be taken in its strongest sense. Jesus was good, with a goodness which would not allow itself to be discouraged by the cowardice of his friends, the disloyalty of those near to him or the wickedness of his adversaries. Even to Judas, who was to betray him, he spoke without hatred or violence. It was a supernatural love, a more than human mercy, distinguished by the most exquisite delicacy, as in the case of the adulteress, to whom not a word of reproach was addressed. And what purity, what transparence there was in this love! Not once do we come across those mental reservations, those egoistic or equivocal elements which spoil so many human feelings.

It is impossible not to feel admiration for a figure like this. By any ethical or psychological criterion, Jesus was certainly as Renan described him, "above the highest peak of human greatness, superior in every way to his disciples . . . an inexhaustible fund of ethical knowledge, the tallest of those columns which show man whence he comes and whither he must aim. In him, all that is good and elevated in our nature is concentrated." Yes, he was the only Master, the only Model, but he was also more than that.

CHAPTER XII

GOD PRESENT IN A MAN

However attentive and devoted anyone seeking to "portray" Jesus may be, he knows very well that he is going to come up against an insurmountable obstacle, that there is a point beyond which comprehension becomes impossible. One reaches the central mystery of his personality, which is also the central mystery of the Christian faith, the mystery of the Incarnation. We cannot talk of Christ as if he were like any other man, even if we regard him as exceptional, as incomparably superior to all the others, for there is something more in him than human verities and powers, something more than genius and holiness, there is the presence of God.

When one has said that, there is really no more to say. To talk of the psychology of Jesus is in a way absurd, since behind the behaviour of the man there is, as a final explanation, the will of God and his power. The mystery of the Incarnation defies analysis; only by prayer and adoration can the holiest souls catch a glimpse of its nature. It is thus not surprising that it is the Incarnation that has attracted the most violent attacks of heretics and unbelievers. That God should be present in a man, a living man, a man of flesh and blood, seemed impossible and almost scandalous to critical minds. To Arius, the Egyptian theologian of the end of the third century, Jesus was not God but a quite exceptional man, with such dazzling virtues that he had been acknowledged to possess the attributes of divinity; other critics said that God had called him to his side, had made him divine at his death.

This line of thought, against which the Church reacted vigorously, particularly in the Council of Nicaea, has reappeared in recent times; in principle, it is the one espoused by Renan, and the admiring phrases which he employs, and which I have quoted, are not without an ulterior meaning. We meet more or less the same ideas in certain aspects of modernism and liberal Protestantism, in the theses of Guignebert, in whose view the "deification" of Jesus was the work of the first generations of Christians. These are the theories to which the Church replies in the simple and definitive words of the Creed: "I believe in Jesus Christ, true God and true man".

Obviously, the presence of God in a man poses innumerable problems. The most important ones can be reduced to these questions: Did Jesus know that he was God? Did he say that he was God? What were the relations in his person between the indissolubly united divine nature and human nature?

We can make a first approach to the mystery by considering the expressions which Jesus uses when he speaks of himself; these expressions were also used by his disciples and later on by the evangelists. In the Hebraic languages, "Son of Man" signified literally, as we have said, a man, a man born of the flesh. But it also signified more than that, in that the expression had overtones transcending the literal interpretation. To a reader of the prophets the phrase "Son of Man" recalled the numerous passages (ninety-four, to be precise) in which Ezechiel uses it to signify a representative of humanity as a whole, a sort of intermediary between humanity and God; or the passage in the Book of Daniel (7. 13) in which, in a grandiose vision, the Son of Man comes "riding on the clouds of heaven" to receive power, glory and sovereignty. For those who had ears to hear, the words "Son of Man" would have a messianic significance, and perhaps a yet greater significance too.

Another parallel expression, "Son of God", may have been more explicit. The evangelists use it a great deal; St Mark even heads his book with it. The Apostles—Peter, for example—use it in speaking of Jesus or to Jesus. Did they attach to it, when their Master was alive, the meaning which the evangelists gave it when they had received the spiritual guarantee of the Resurrection, the Ascension and Pentecost? For the Israelites, the people of the Covenant, to be the "son of God" was a general characteristic. "You are the children of Yahweh, your God," Moses had said to them (Deut. 14. 1). But other passages in the Bible seem to give it a more precise meaning; Psalm 2, for example, which makes Yahweh say to an interlocutor who seems to be the Messias: "Thou art my son; I have begotten thee this day. Ask thy will of me, and thou shalt have the nations for thy patrimony; the very ends of the world for thy domain." So when they spoke of the "Son of God", the disciples of Jesus meant to recognize that he was the Messias.

Did they recognize anything more? Did they use the expression in the sense made explicit by St Paul when he wrote: "God has sent us his own Son, in the fashion of our guilty nature" (Rom. 8. 3)? And did Jesus himself accept the phrase as implying that the mystery of God was really present in him? We must seek the answer to this question in the behaviour of Jesus and in his own words.

Surprising as it may seem, the miracles performed by Jesus did not constitute, in the eyes of a Jew of his age, proof of his divinity or even of his messianic character.[1] Scripture recorded a good number of miracles which could be considered just as impressive as Christ's. Making manna fall from heaven in the middle of the desert or causing water to gush forth from the rock of Horeb, as Moses had done, was just as striking as multiplying loaves or changing water into wine. As for healing the sick, or even raising the dead, prophets like Elias and Eliseus had done this, and no one had thought that they were God or even the Messias. Even the wonder of the Trans-

[1] This profound observation was made by Fr Lagrange, the founder of the Biblical School at Jerusalem.

figuration, which in the context of the Christian revelation seems the most dazzling of theophanies, probably did not seem so convincing to the three Jews who witnessed it if they remembered the supernatural light which radiated from Moses' forehead when he came down from Sinai. All these things made Jesus seem like the repository of the divine power, but not necessarily the "Son of God", God living on earth.

However, other elements in his person and his message allow us to go much further. The first of these is his moral conduct. It is not enough to say, like Renan, that by his virtues Jesus is the archetype of all perfection, although this alone brings him near to the attributes of God; we have to recognize that he was, in the etymological sense of the word, an extraordinary man, one immune from the liability to sin. It is clear that Jesus assumed every aspect of the human condition except complicity with evil. The greatest saints have sinned, and recognized that they were sinners. But one cannot cite a single gesture or thought of Jesus which is not in full accord with the divine law. "Can any of you convict me of sin?" To utter a challenge like that without fear of contradiction, one must be either mad or God.

Jesus' relations with God are no less revealing. When he speaks of him to the Apostles, he says, "Your Father"; when he teaches them, and all mankind, the most perfect of prayers, he identifies himself with humanity and says "Our Father"; but when he refers to his own personal relations with God, when he interprets God's will to man, he says, "My Father". It is the phrase which he had already employed, as a small boy, when he replied to his parents at the time of the incident in the Temple. For him it clearly implies a sacred intimacy in comparison with which earthly affections, even the most legitimate ones, are only secondary.

This is the explanation of something which, we know, amazed the witnesses of his mission: "He taught them, not like their scribes and Pharisees, but like one who had authority" (Matt. 7. 28-9; Mark 1. 22). He does not conform to the framework of traditional rabbinical teaching; he does not support his arguments with references to the masters, as every good rabbi did. He speaks with authority; hence his attitude to the Law. So far as what the Law teaches expresses the will of God, it is holy and meant to be followed in every detail; but it is not the same with the rest, with what has been added by men. And it is Jesus who distinguishes between the two. The Son of Man is master of the Law; "fulfilling" or perfecting it is part of his divine mission. Good examples of this are his reminder that the spirit of charity is more important than the tithe of cumin and fennel, and his deliberate disregard of hair-splitting Sabbath observances. Indeed, his reply to those who reproach him for healing a man on the Sabbath day contains a comparison which suggests a far-reaching identification: "My Father has never ceased working, and I too must be at work" (John 5. 17).

Jesus encroaches still more obviously on territory reserved to God when he forgives sins. Only God can read hearts and minds—Jeremias had stressed that (17, 9, 10)—only God has the right and the power to absolve men's faults. Yet Jesus arrogates this right to himself. He even makes it clear that for him it is as easy to say to a paralytic "Thy sins are forgiven thee" as "Arise and walk". If he did not carry within himself the certainty that he was God, such behaviour would be quite pointless.

Did Jesus communicate to others this secret that he carried in his heart? That is, did he assert not only that he was the Messias but also that he was the "Son of God", God himself? It is not easy to answer this question. When we read the gospels today, that is, in the full light of Revelation, we find a considerable number of phrases in them which seem to hint at Jesus' great secret. For example, he says to his followers, "there have been many prophets and just men who have longed to see what you see, to hear what you hear" (Matt. 13. 16, 17; Luke 10. 23–4); he declares, "a greater than Solomon is here" (Matt. 12. 42; Luke 11. 22); and "Before Abraham was, I am" (John 8. 58); and he asserts that heaven and earth will pass away, but his words will not pass away (Matt. 24. 35). Further examples could easily be produced; in all of these cases we can really hear God speaking. Was this as clear to those around Jesus, to those who saw him daily, who had before their eyes the carpenter's son from Nazareth, the leader of the little band of Galilean fishermen torn away from their nets?

We must also take into account the obvious precautions taken by Jesus to prevent the truth about himself from appearing too quickly, and to prevent his faithful followers from interpreting his displays of power erroneously. We have seen that he disclosed part of his secret to a foreign woman whom he had met by chance, and to a member of the Sanhedrin who would clearly not talk about it. As for his closest followers, he does not hide it from them, but he does not proclaim it to them either, confining himself to congratulating Simon Peter on the inspiration from above which impelled him to call Jesus "Son of God". Again and again, on the other hand, after a particularly impressive miracle and after the charisma of the Transfiguration, he insists on their keeping silence. The idea of a progressive revelation of his godhead intended and decided by Jesus is absolutely fundamental. The devils were the first to shout out in public who it was who had vanquished them (Mark 1. 24 and 3. 11), and this was no accident.

However, the moment was to come when Jesus had to disclose the truth about himself one way or the other. On the tragic night of the trial, when the High Priest asked him if he was the Messias, the son of the Most High, he replied without the slightest ambiguity, for by then it was a question of putting the seal on the new revelation, of accepting all the risks entailed in his mission.

There can thus be no doubt: the divinity in the man Jesus was not a sort of unconscious power which he used without realizing it. Messias and more than Messias, the living God, he knew that he was "one with the father" (John 10. 30) and that "no one had been God's interpreter but the Son, who abides in the bosom of the Father" (John 1. 18). But his friends and those near to him only knew the whole truth when everything had been accomplished.

The third question belongs not so much to the realm of psychology—the term is completely out of place in this context—as to metaphysics or something near it. Can we form any notion of the relations in the person of Jesus between his human nature and his divine nature? The gospels do give us a few succinct indications on the subject, which in fact lies beyond the scope of explanation.

On several occasions we receive the impression that the divine power takes hold of Jesus' person, lifts it up, fills it with a mysterious joy. St Luke depicts him "filled with gladness by the Holy Spirit" when he utters a splendid prayer in which he says: "My Father has entrusted everything into my hands; none knows what the Son is, except the Father, and none knows what the Father is, except the Son" (Luke 10. 21; Matt. 11. 5–27). Similarly, when he is about to set the divine power in action to raise Lazarus, Jesus is troubled; in the words of St John, "he sighed to himself" (John 11. 33). A still more curious hint is given in the account of the cure of the woman with a haemorrhage; at the moment when the sick woman touches the fringe at the back of his tunic, Jesus turns and asks, "Who touched me? I can tell that power has gone out from me" (Matt. 9; Mark 5; Luke 8).

But there were also moments, one suspects, when there was not quite opposition, but tension between the two natures in Jesus. That is the fundamental meaning of the Temptation: Jesus' divine vocation rises superior to what could be a vocation to earthly success. The tension was particularly great when the divine vocation obliged the man of flesh and blood to accept a fate involving sacrifice. The sober exclamation recorded by St Luke tells us much about the hidden drama which must have been enacted in a conscience no different from our own: "I must receive another baptism, and I am impatient for its accomplishment!" (Luke 12. 50). In Gethsemani the tension was so great that for a moment Jesus nearly failed in his mission by asking his Father to "take away this chalice"; but he regained control of himself at once, his divine vocation rose superior to the fear felt by his human nature, and he exclaimed, "Not my will, Father, but thine." For he knew, with his divine foreknowledge, that the Son of God had come on earth to suffer and to die as a man, and if he escaped this fate by supernatural means all he had come to say and do on earth would have been vain.

CHAPTER XIII

IN BLEAK JUDAEA

Autumn of the year 29 saw the opening of a new chapter in Jesus' career. He left Galilee and entered Judaea, where he was to remain from now onwards—except for two trips across the Jordan to Peraea—until the end. Why did he take this decision? It is unlikely that he yielded to the unambiguous advice of some of his relatives, who were probably anxious to rid their district of a presence which they regarded as embarrassing (John 7. 1–6). He probably thought that his mission in Galilee had borne the fruits he expected from it. But, at a deeper level, St Luke gives the real reason for this change of locality: "And now the time was drawing near for his taking away from the earth, and he turned his eyes steadfastly towards the way that led to Jerusalem" (Luke 9. 51).

There is thus a link, transcending any human explanation, between the new area of evangelization and the destiny which awaited Jesus there. "There is no room for a prophet to meet his death, except at Jerusalem," he said, as though it were something which was self-evident and admitted no discussion (Luke 13. 33). Judaea was associated in his plans with the sacrificial vocation, fulfilled by suffering and death, to which he had already alluded.

Besides, he could hardly have deluded himself about the opposition which he was likely to meet in this new area, an opposition much stronger and better organized than that in Galilee. Judaea and Jerusalem were the bastions of the Law, the land of strict observances, of the most eminent doctors.

It was also the region where the problem of relations with the occupying power arose in its sharpest form, causing frequent anxiety to the Jewish community's fragile theocratic government, which was always fearful that a change in the mood of the Romans might jeopardize its rights. When he entered Judaea with its bare rocks, barren hills and desolate ravines, so different from his native Galilee, Jesus knew very well what risks he was taking.

In essentials, this Judaean period of Christ's mission does not differ from the preceding one. Jesus remains the same, healing, comforting and dealing out the same sublime teaching in his discourses, informal conversations and parables. However, it is possible to observe a difference of emphasis in his attitude. In Judaea he no longer performs the "charming miracles", the purely human marvels exemplified in the Galilean period by the changing of the water into wine, the multiplication of the loaves or the miraculous draught of fishes. Instead, he lays emphasis in his teaching on messianic themes, as though to try to make those around him understand what his real rôle was, and at the same time to stress the incomprehension which he met on every side. We seem to detect in him a sort of holy impatience caused both by the resistance he encounters, the hatred he senses, and the approach of the final catastrophe with which his infinite foreknowledge has already made him familiar. It was in this Judaean period that he uttered the mysterious sentence, "It is fire that I have come to spread over the earth, and what better wish can I have than that it should be kindled?" (Luke 12. 49). This is the bright flame of love of which the mystics were to speak, a flame which should be devouring, but is allowed to burn so low by men.

All the episodes recorded by the Gospel in connection with this period give the same impression, namely that the Word is falling among a people divided and, like the seed that fell on stony ground in the parable of the Sower, will find difficulty in taking root. We sense that Jesus knows this, that it pains him, and that it impels him to adopt a more urgent tone.

So we find him at Jerusalem during the feast of Tents, also known as the feast of Tabernacles. It was celebrated about October 15th, when work on the land was over, at the beginning of the legal year. A week before, the People had rid itself of its sins, during the penitential feast of *Yom Kippur*, by chasing the "scapegoat" into the desert. A reminder of the long wanderings of their forefathers, the feast of Tents was a very joyful one. You had to leave your house and live in a hut made of leaves. You went up to the Temple waving in one hand the *lulab*, a bundle of palm leaves, and in the other the *ethrog*, a bunch of citrons. Alleluias rang out ceaselessly. There were big ceremonies, such as the one in which the High Priest, followed by all the men, went to draw water from the pool of Siloe. In the evening, the Temple was lit up by thousands of torches carried by all those present, with the two sacred candlesticks, which were fifty cubits high, over-topping the whole scene.

Jesus goes up to the Temple and speaks in the colonnades, like the other rabbis. He takes great pains to indicate just what his position is to these audiences who do not know him. "The learning which I impart", he says, "is not my own, it comes from him who sent me" (John 7. 16). Making use of the imagery before the eyes of his listeners—the holy water, the flames in the night—he exclaims: "If any man is thirsty, let him come to me and drink"; and again, "I am the light of the world. He who follows me can never walk in darkness; he will possess the light which is life" (John 8. 12). What was the result of these assertions? St John, who reports the events carefully in his Gospel, does not hide the fact that reactions were far from being unanimously favourable. Some people were amazed; how could he speak like this, they asked, without being a scribe? (John 7. 15). Others were decidedly hostile and told those who supported Jesus that he was leading the people astray (John 7. 11, 12). There were certainly some who were won over, convinced, but on the whole public opinion was worried, divided and rather hostile (John 7. 26–46). Thus the atmosphere in which the final act was to be played gradually built up.

It is a striking fact that it was precisely in this period and in this atmosphere that Jesus showed his immense goodness most clearly in word and deed. It is here that we can see most clearly the heart of Christ and the charity of Christ. They emerge not only in his miracles—the healing of a congenitally blind man and of a leper, incidents in which his actions are as sensitive as they are effective—but also in his attitude and in his teaching.

It was in the Judaean period that the revealing episode of the woman taken in adultery took place (John 8. 1–11). She had been caught *in flagrante delicto,* and in such a case the Law was categorical: the guilty woman had to be stoned. The Scribes and Pharisees brought her to Jesus, obviously to set a trap for him. They asked him if he agreed that the sentence should be carried out immediately, hoping to see whether he would dare to oppose the Law or contradict the universal charity which he preached. Jesus' answer showed a profound knowledge of the human heart. He was silent for some time, tracing in the sand of the road signs that he alone understood, then he straightened up and spoke: "Whichever of you is free from sin shall cast the first stone at her." The evangelist adds, possibly with a trace of irony, that those present started to go away one by one, beginning with the eldest.

It is also Christ's charity that strikes us most if we think about the lessons of the great parables which he told during these weeks in Judaea and Peraea. It was then that he made the famous comparison between himself and the Good Shepherd, the man who knows his sheep and whose sheep know him, who guards and protects them (John 10. 7–18). It was then, too, that continuing the comparison with the shepherd, he told the story of the man who leaves the rest of his sheep behind to look for the one that is lost, and rejoices greatly

when he finds it (Luke 15. 4–7; Matt. 18. 12). This lesson is
repeated in another parable, that of the small coin lost under
a piece of furniture and sought anxiously and eagerly by the
mistress of the house. This is a very comforting lesson for
sinners, for whom, as Jesus reminds them, in God's infinite
mercy there is always particular care and attention. Still more
moving is the parable of the Prodigal Son, related only by
St Luke (15. 11–32), whom Dante called "the scribe of God's
forbearance". What sinner has not felt that he himself is this
child who has betrayed and abandoned the love of his Father,
yet finds him there, at the hour of repentance, with open
arms and words of forgiveness on his lips, as every man
would like to find God on the Day of Judgement?

An immense appeal for love and charity is embodied in
Jesus' teaching during this period. When a doctor of the Law
asked him which the greatest commandment was, he replied,
"Love God and love thy neighbour", the two things being
identical. When the doctor pressed him, clumsily trying to set
another trap, and asked who one's neighbour was, he replied
with the parable of the Good Samaritan, the heretic who
showed himself true neighbour to the wounded man by the
roadside whom no pious Jew had helped. Charity must be
boundless, undiscriminating and universal (Luke 10. 25–37).

The culminating point of Jesus' mission in Judaea was
almost certainly the day, perhaps in October, 29, when, in
response to a formal request from his disciples, he taught
them how to pray. It may have been on the Mount of Olives,
or perhaps on "Ephraim's balcony", with its lovely view. He
responded, then, to his disciples' plea, and there fell from
human lips for the first time the prayer which so many men
were to repeat down the centuries as a pledge of their faith
and a sign of their hope, the Lord's Prayer.

It is a sublime prayer, summarizing all that man can say
to God, all that he can ask of him. It is a touching prayer, so
near to man's daily cares, so confident in God's infinite mercy,
so full of love. It is a mystical prayer, each of whose verses

awakens an echo in the Scriptures and suggests infinite
mysteries. It is a wonderfully simple prayer—so different from
the Jews' lengthy *Eighteen Benedictions*—a prayer that every
man in every age can understand and say. It sums up Christ's
whole message, in language of radiant purity.

So all is not tension and disquiet in this Judaean period,
which was to end in the most terrible of dramas. It would be
a mistake to think of Jesus as surrounded only by distrust and
suspicion turning quickly into jealousy and hatred. In Judaea,
as in Galilee, we find a number of faithful followers round
the young master, men and women full of confidence in his
teaching and of devotion to his person. Some of the most
touching episodes in the Gospel take place in Judaea. A good
example is the one in which Jesus is shown surrounded by
little children, making them welcome, patting their heads and
profiting by the incident to give a definitive lesson to the
adults present on the "childlike spirit" which shall inherit the
Kingdom (Matt. 19. 13–15; Mark 10. 13–16; Luke 3. 15–17).
Another example is that of Zacchaeus, the publican of Jericho,
who wanted to meet Christ but did not dare to approach him
because he knew the contempt in which all publicans were
held. Being a short man, he climbed up into a sycamore tree
to catch a glimpse of Jesus. Jesus saw him from a distance
and did him the honour of asking if he might lodge with him
(Luke 19. 1–10).

One of Jesus' friendships in the Judaean months occupies
a special place in the Gospel. This is his friendship with a
whole family—two sisters and a brother, at any rate—who
lived at Bethany, a little township a short distance to the east
of Jerusalem. We receive the impression that Jesus often
stayed in this friendly house, that he regarded it as a place of
rest, a stop between his evangelizing trips. Several scenes
from Jesus' private life at Bethany are known to us, and they
do not lack significance. One day—he had probably just
arrived—one of the two sisters, Martha, was busy preparing

the mats in his room and the food for his meal, but the other, Mary, just sat at the Master's feet listening to him. Martha was surprised, almost angry, at her sister's behaviour, but Christ's response was a rather strange lesson; he said that Mary, the meditative, contemplative sister, had "chosen the better part". It was an imperious reminder of the hierarchy of values: prayer, meditation is more important than the performance of innumerable jobs; it is "the one thing necessary" (Luke 10. 38–42).

It was also for the family at Bethany that Jesus performed one of his most striking miracles. While the Master was away on one occasion, the son, Lazarus, fell ill and died. When Christ returned he found the house in mourning. Humanly speaking, all was over; Lazarus had been dead for three days and corruption was already setting in; the sisters could only express their sadness to Jesus. But Jesus went to the tomb and caused it to be opened. Then came the wonderful, the incredible scene: the dead man, still tied up with strips of linen, walked out of the tomb. None of the other resurrections effected by Jesus had the spectacular, overwhelming character of this one (John 11. 1–53).

So Jesus had some great friendships in Judaea, but he also provoked more and more mistrust and hatred. Indeed, according to St John, the raising of Lazarus was one of the major reasons which induced his opponents to decide to get rid of him. He himself knew that his hour was approaching. On several occasions he alluded to it quite clearly. One of these occasions was in the house at Bethany, during the course of a probably rather special meal; the women did not take their places at the table but served the food. Mary, behaving in her usual way, was thinking of anything but the meal itself. Going up to Jesus with a jar of ointment, she anointed either his hair (according to St Matthew and St Mark) or his feet (according to St John). The same thing had been done earlier on in Galilee by a sinful woman whom one tradition identifies with Mary of Bethany. A voice protested, that of the disciple who kept the common purse; he was indignant at the waste. But Jesus made this reply: "This woman has done well. She has anointed my body beforehand to prepare it for burial" (John 12. 2–3; Mark 14. 3–9). It was a terrible presage. Another was still clearer; it came on the Jericho road, when Jesus was going up to Jerusalem with his disciples for the last time. He called the twelve Apostles to his side and said to them: "The son of Man will be given up into the hands of the chief priests and scribes. They will condemn him to death and hand him over to the Gentiles, who will mock him, and spit upon him; but on the third day he will rise again" (Mark 10. 32–4; Matt. 20. 17–19; Luke 18. 31–4).

Nothing could be more explicit than this announcement. Was it understood? Henceforth, did those who were closely associated with Christ's work have a better understanding of the adventure through which they were living, of the words which they heard? It does not seem so. We find two of the Apostles—Andrew and John—letting their mother, Salome, make a misplaced request to Jesus—on the pretext that she has helped Jesus with her goods—for two choice positions for her sons in the kingdom which he is clearly going to set up! (Matt. 20. 20–4; Mark 10. 35–41). Men's blindness continues. Jesus is not angry; he simply replies, "The Son of Man did not come to have service done him; he came to serve others, and to give his life as a ransom for the lives of many" (Matt. 20. 20–8; Mark 10. 45). The time was coming when all would be horribly clear even to the most hopelessly blind.

CHAPTER XIV

"IT IS BETTER THAT ONE MAN SHOULD DIE..."

Jesus' mission in Judaea soon provoked a reaction. It was no longer in a remote region that he was preaching his paradoxical message, among people who had the reputation for being not very well informed in matters of religion and doctrinally somewhat unsound. In Jerusalem and the surrounding district a large number of people prided themselves on knowing the Law thoroughly and obeying it in every detail. A nonconformist was bound to arouse discussions and retorts.

The Fourth Gospel, which is particularly precise about the events of this period, shows very clearly how the opposition to Jesus crystallized, grew and finally ended in the murderous decision to get rid of him. The process began with discussions about him between those who were attracted by him and those who remained mistrustful. "Some of the multitude, who had heard him, said, Beyond doubt, this is the prophet. Others said, This is the Christ; and others again, Is the Christ, then, to come from Galilee? Has not the scripture told us that Christ is to come from the family of David, and from the village of Bethlehem, where David lived?" (John 7. 40–3).

The leaders of the Jewish community were on the alert; some people were surprised that they let the prophet speak freely; had they recognized him as the Messias? (John 7. 26). They had to act, but how? If it was only a question of some little agitator, of one of these self-styled prophets who were always turning up, a very small-scale police operation might be enough; a few Temple policemen mingling with the crowd would find a means of noting some offence and of arresting the speaker. But the operation failed; the constables returned so impressed by Jesus that they had not dared to lay a finger on him (John 7. 46).

Tension increased from week to week, and all the evidence suggests that Jesus made no effort to prevent it from increasing. It even looks as if he made a special point of snapping his fingers at the formalism and legalism of the Jews at Jerusalem. When he restored a blind man's sight, he performed the miracle on the Sabbath and performed it with a piece of thaumaturgy—the application of mud to the eyelids—which was certainly forbidden by the jurisprudence of the doctors of the Law (John 9. 1–7). When some doctors were angry and protested, they received a sharp lesson from Jesus about the existence of other blindnesses besides that of the flesh (John 9. 13–41). A similar incident is reported by St Luke (13. 10–17) in connection with a woman knotted with rheumatism whom Jesus put on her feet, again on the Sabbath.

There were many other points in Jesus' teaching which must have caused discontent and anger. On many questions he adopted an attitude contrary not only to the traditional teaching but even, so it seemed, to the Mosaic Law itself. For example, in the matter of marriage, where divorce was permitted so long as certain guarantees about the lot of the woman repudiated were given, Jesus proclaimed that "no man was to separate what God had joined together" (Matt. 19. 3; Mark 2. 12; Luke 16. 18). Was this, then, what he meant, people asked, when he spoke of "fulfilling the Law"?

It was ordained that everything about Jesus' message should offend the susceptibilities of the traditionalists. For centuries Judaea had considered itself the bulwark of the proudest Israelite nationalism and the most jealous religious fidelity; the two things were in fact identical. How curiously insistent Jesus was in suggesting that the Chosen People would not have sole right of entry to the Kingdom of Heaven! Why did he speak so often of these prodigal sons, of these lost sheep who had as much right to the Master's love as faithful believers? Why did he depict Samaritans, who were so detestable to an Israelite, in morally nobler situations than practising Jews? Did the only leper who showed gratitude and the only charitable traveller in the parable have to be Samaritans? Jesus' words were sometimes even positively insulting to Jewish ears: "You will have to die with your sins upon you; you belong to earth, I to heaven" (John 8. 21–5). In other words, you can understand nothing.

It was hardly surprising that discussions grew frequent and heated; that he was accused of being a mere magician, an agent of the devil (John 8. 49); and that some impetuous persons even stoned him. In some circles people began to ask whether following the Galilean was not a crime demanding an exemplary punishment, perhaps the *herem,* formal exclusion from the synagogue.

During the winter of 29–30 discussion of "the Jesus case" certainly grew more serious and reached the higher levels of the Jewish community. When Nicodemus, a member of the Sanhedrin, who had not forgotten his conversation with the young Messias, remarked to his colleagues, justly and sensibly, that before condemning a man they ought to hear him and find out exactly what he was accused of, he drew sarcastic comments such as "Art thou, too, from Galilee?" (John 7. 50–2). The atmosphere normal in disputes of this sort was building up: any sensible remark makes the person who utters it suspect to the fanatics on both sides.

Thus was accomplished the prediction made many years before by that holy old man Simeon, when, in the courts of the Temple, he had recognized in a little boy cradled in his mother's arms "the light which would dissipate the darkness, the glory of Israel"; for he had added, "This child will be a sign which men will refuse to acknowledge" (Luke 2. 29–35).

At this point, when the refusal was about to become obvious, there is one question which we cannot help asking: Was the refusal inevitable? Was there bound to be opposition between Jesus and God's Chosen People?

The opposition was at any rate not connected with the person of Jesus, with the man as he appeared to his audiences. As the French poet Péguy rightly said to his Jewish friends: "He was a Jew, an ordinary Jew, a Jew like yourselves, a Jew among other Jews." We have already seen that in his daily behaviour, his clothes, his food, the languages he spoke, he was a genuine Palestinian Jew like any other. His style of speech, his parables, were typical of Jewish oratory. And like a faithful Jew he always based his arguments on passages from Scripture.

Was the content of his message less admissible than its form? On many essential points he was in full accord with his people; for example, when he reaffirmed Israel's vocation and told the Samaritan woman, "Salvation comes from the Jews"; or when he proclaimed the immutability of the Law revealed to Israel, "not one jot of which would disappear", and which no one could transgress without closing the Kingdom of Heaven to himself (Matt. 5. 17–19). Besides, he himself could be seen submitting to the Law and the customs of his people, fasting, praying and making the pilgrimage up to Jerusalem for the principal feasts.

Many of the elements in his teaching were traditional ones. For centuries Israel had learnt to love God "above all things", and that God was the supreme perfection whom one should aim to imitate. Jesus' command, "You are to be perfect, as your heavenly Father is perfect" (Matt. 5. 48), was almost a quotation from the Bible (Levit. 11. 44; 19. 2; 20. 26; 21. 6). God's love for men, on which Jesus laid much emphasis, speaking often of God's fatherhood, was not unknown to the Jewish tradition, even if in recent times Israel had tended, from an excess of respect, to place God at a great distance from man, to make him inaccessibly transcendent.

Even Jesus' ethical system, which may have seemed the
most astonishing element in his teaching, had deep roots in
the tradition of Israel. "Love thy neighbour as thyself" was a
precept of the Mosaic Law (Levit. 19. 17, 18). "Do to others
what you would have them do to you" (Matt. 7. 12) was more
or less what old Tobias had taught (Tobias 4. 16). A more
inward, more truthful moral and religious life was what the
great prophets had taught. Isaias in particular (58. 6, 7) had
declared that the kind of fasting which was pleasing to God
did not consist in covering one's head with ashes, but in showing oneself charitable and generous. Even in the teaching of
certain doctors of the Pharisees—Rabbi Hillel and Rabbi
Gamaliel, for example—one could find elements curiously
similar to some of the things which Jesus taught. There are
precepts in the Talmud which are just the same as those of
Jesus: "Charity is above the Law"; "It is not contact with
death that makes one impure, but sin, and it is not water that
purifies. . . ."

In many respects, then, Jesus seems to have been right in
the main stream of Jewish tradition, the culmination, as it
were, of the ancient message which had been elaborated down
the centuries. Yet there was a conflict between him and his
people, and it was a fundamental one. It concerned a number
of points of unequal importance. The most serious of these
was that Jesus presented himself as the bearer of a new
message—the new wine which was not to be put in old
bottles—and that consequently he and his supporters asserted
that they were the true heirs to Israel's divine calling. Phrases
like "You have been taught until now, but I tell you" or "All
the prophets and the Law have taught up to John's time"
were shocking to Jewish ears. When a supercilious Jew heard
the resounding declaration, "I have not come to set aside the
Law, but to perfect it," it would be the last part of the sentence that he would remember, and he would be scandalized
by it. He would find it difficult to believe that the Holy Law
could be deepened or perfected; it was so immutable and

definitive that some rabbis taught that God himself revered and obeyed it. The very idea of a new Revelation was unacceptable to anyone who did not agree to effect that "second birth", mention of which had so astonished Nicodemus.

This Revelation was all the more unacceptable because Jesus did not restrict it to the Chosen People alone. We have seen how much Israel's touchy nationalism was offended by Jesus' too kindly allusions to Samaritans, prodigal sons and workers of the eleventh hour, who all, so he said, were entitled to the Father's mercy. Israelite tradition had certainly included a universalist current, according to which all men could be entitled to salvation, but it had encountered violent opposition. Other people besides Jonas had been indignant at the idea of the Ninevites receiving the word of God. In Israelite tradition, one's neighbour was one's brother by blood and by religion, not the *goy,* the foreigner. "To you alone I have given my name," Yahweh had said. The *Kahal,* the community of believers, bound together by a whole series of spiritual and temporal interests, could only admit, at the most, Gentiles who "feared God", that is, who had agreed to submit to the Law; the concept of a Church, based on the union of all who share in the divine grace, was totally different.

The opposition was thus a good deal more substantial than might have appeared from the bitter discussions about the Sabbath and other observances. However, it must be understood that in stressing the rigidity of precepts, in "raising the hedge of the Law", as the Pharisees put it, the Jews could take the view that they were obeying a sacred duty. Literalism carried to the extreme in every petty detail may seem to us absurd, but we must not forget that it was this total fidelity to the Law which had enabled the Jewish people to survive and to avoid absorption by the pagans all round them. To leave these observances behind and live by grace, illumined only by the Holy Spirit, was a leap into the unknown of a kind that very few men are bold enough to take; people usually prefer the comforting crutches of legal observances and established rituals.

Only one factor could have prevented the opposition between Jesus and his people from ending in a dramatic conflict, and that was his recognition as the Messias, God's envoy, from whom one could receive the ultimate revelation. But apart from the fact that Jesus, as we have seen, made no visible effort to have himself officially recognized as the Messias, the very appearances under which he presented himself were such as to hinder any such recognition. It cannot be emphasized too often that it was natural for a long-humiliated people to think of the providential being described in the Scriptures as a powerful leader who would restore Israel's glory. The few passages of the Bible which spoke of a suffering Messias, sacrificed for the salvation of mankind, only took on their true meaning in the light of the Christian revelation. If the announcement, repeated several times by Jesus, of his ignominious death on the cross was known, it must have scandalized people, and in any case persuaded them that he could not be the promised Messias.

Thus the reasons which the leaders of the Jewish community had for putting a swift end to Jesus' mission were profound and serious. They concerned what counted most for the Jews, religious realities. However, it seems that it was not this kind of reason which was invoked in favour of taking action. After the raising of Lazarus, which obviously could not have passed unnoticed, there was a meeting, described by St John (11. 45–53); no doubt it was followed by others. Pontiffs, priests and doctors of the Law took part in them.

"What are we to do?" they said. "This man is performing a large number of miracles. If we let him carry on, the masses will believe in him. After which the Romans will come and destroy our people." We must be honest and recognize that the danger was not an imaginary one. Under the influence of religious agitators, the Jewish people had already allowed ítself several times to indulge in rebellions which the Romans had sternly repressed. People still remembered the two thousand crosses set up by Varus on Mt Scopus after the revolt of Simon the shepherd. Caiphas, the reigning High Priest, was adopting a prudent policy when he gave it as his opinion that it was better to put one man to death than to see the whole nation perish. So it was for reasons of State that action was to be taken against Jesus. He was arrested, not because he proclaimed himself the Messias, the Son of God, and was shaking the religious foundations of Israel, but because he was provoking agitation which might have serious consequences. But when it made this decision the council of chief priests and doctors of the Law was surely, without realizing it, the instrument of Providence. St John reminds us that during his term of office the High Priest enjoyed the gift of prophecy. Caiphas had foretold the future of God.

CHAPTER XV

THE NISAN MOON

Of all the feasts in the Israelite calendar the holiest and most fervently observed was the Passover or Pasch. Since the days of Moses it had recalled the deliverance of God's People from slavery in Egypt, and the signs of particular good will which the Lord had given his followers on that occasion. It was in memory of the events recounted in the Book of Exodus that the Jews sacrificed the paschal lamb, sprinkled its blood on the lintels and jambs of their doors with the aid of a branch of hyssop, and ate the animal's flesh with unleavened bread.

Jesus decided to go up to Jerusalem to celebrate the Passover there; for a Jew, this was a mark of piety. The evangelists have recorded the fact, all four making it quite clear that the death of Jesus took place on the Friday on which, at nightfall, the ceremonies of the Passover began (see, for example, John 18. 28). Since it was laid down that the Passover was to be celebrated on the fourteenth day of the (lunar) month of Nisan, and since the 14 Nisan fell on Friday in the year 30, it seems reasonable to regard the April 7th, 30 as the tragic Friday, the "Good Friday" of Christian tradition.

So the last week which Jesus was to pass on earth began on Sunday, April 2nd. It was a strangely full week, mysteriously marked by a succession of light and dark patches, and ending in the night of Golgotha and the Sepulchre, then the glorious morning of the Resurrection. It is the week which the liturgy, following the Gospel account step by step, accompanies with the solemn rites of "Holy Week". Christ is still

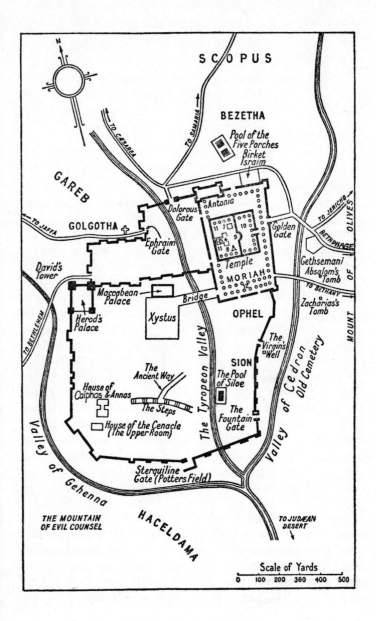

N

S C O P U S

BEZETHA

Pool of the
Five Porches
Birket
Israim

GAREB

TO SAMARIA

TO CAESAREA

Dolorous
Gate

Antonia

GOLGOTHA

TO JAFFA

Ephraim
Gate

11 7 □ 10

6 5
11 8 4

9

Golden
Gate

TO JERICHO

BETHPHAGE

MOUNT OF OLIVES

TO BETHANY

Temple

MORIAH

Gethsemani
Absalom's
Tomb

David's
Tower

Maccabean
Palace

Bridge

OPHEL

Zacharias's
Tomb

TO BETHLEHEM

Herod's
Palace

Xystus

SION

The
Virgin's
Well

The Pool
of Siloe

House of
Caiphas & Annas

The
Ancient Way

The Steps

The Tyropeon Valley

The
Fountain
Gate

Valley of Cedron

Old Cemetery

House of the Cenacle
(The Upper Room)

Valley of Gehenna

Sterquiline
Gate (Potters Field)

THE MOUNTAIN
OF EVIL COUNSEL

HACELDAMA

TO JUDAEAN
DESERT

Scale of Yards

0   100 200 300 400 500

present on earth for a few days; he takes up several of the essential themes of his message; he shows his power again; he utters a few terrible warnings. Above all, he advances towards the total sacrifice which he has desired and predicted, the sacrifice which will give his mission on earth its full significance. Meanwhile, the new moon of Nisan climbs the pearly sky; it will be full, on the evening of Holy Thursday, above the olive trees of Gethsemani.

The week began in striking fashion. Jesus had no doubt been staying at Bethany, and he set out for Jerusalem on the Sunday morning. His disciples and a number of his followers were with him. On the way he met people who had come out from the city, in accordance with ancient custom, to meet pilgrims coming up for the Passover. They made quite a little crowd.

Just before arriving at the top of the Mount of Olives Jesus stopped. There was a village there, Bethphage, "the house of figs", and it was market day. "Go into the village," said Jesus, "and untie a she-ass and a foal that you will find there, and bring them to me. If anyone raises an objection, say that the Lord has need of them, and you will be allowed to take the animals" (Matt. 21. 1–7; Mark 11. 1–7; Luke 19. 29–35). The command seems rather strange to the modern reader, but it would have seemed much less so to the Jews round Jesus. Even if the mode of borrowing the she-ass was unusual, one could sense that it had a prophetic significance. After all, Zacharias had said: "See where thy king comes to greet thee, a trusty deliverer; see how lowly he rides, mounted on an ass, the foal of an ass" (9. 9). A messianic entry was being arranged.

Such was certainly the scene that actually took place. "The moment", says Romano Guardini, "belongs to the power of the Spirit." Jesus arrived, in the sunshine of the Palestinian spring, in sight of the city. His friends and followers acclaimed him, and there was soon a whole crowd surging round him. It should not be forgotten that there were hundreds of thousands of pilgrims camping round Jerusalem at this time. "Who is it?" asked those loitering by the roadside. "Jesus, the prophet from Nazareth in Galilee", was the answer, and Hosannas rang out, people cut branches off the palm trees and waved them enthusiastically above their heads, and cloaks were strewn on the ground to make a ceremonial carpet for the Messias' mount (Matt. 21. 4–9; Mark 11. 8–10; Luke 14. 36–8; John 12. 12–18). A curious triumph, which was to remain limited and modest, but a significant one; now that the hour of decision was at hand, Jesus no longer needed to keep his messianic character half-concealed; indeed, it was important that it should be recognized.

However, amid these manifestations of joy Jesus had a deep feeling of anxiety and anguish. When he arrived on the crest of the Mount of Olives, he stopped; the city lay before him, behind huge walls bristling with towers, looking invincible and eternal. But the power of the Holy Spirit gave Christ a quite different picture, that of a Jerusalem besieged, crushed and destroyed (Luke 19. 41–4). Why? Because it had been blind to the light. Everything was falling into place; it was not only the distant drama of the capture of Jerusalem by the Roman legions that Jesus saw, but also his own personal drama, now quite near. St John even notes that, for a moment, he was shaken by this certainty: "And now my soul is disturbed. What am I to say? I will say, Father, save me from undergoing this hour of trial." It was only a passing thought, a very human weakness. He took hold of himself again at once: "And yet, I have only reached this hour of trial that I might undergo it" (John 12. 27). He repeated to his followers the lesson he had already given them often: "The time has come now for the Son of Man to achieve his glory. Believe me when I tell you this; a grain of wheat must fall into the ground and die, or else it remains nothing more than a grain of wheat; but if it dies, then it yields rich fruit" (John 12. 23–4).

He entered the city and the enthusiasm in the streets was also great. Even Gentiles asked to be introduced to him.

Groups of children crowded round the prophet. The anger of the opposing faction rose: "What is the good of hesitating? Everyone is running after him!" When he arrived at the Temple, the goal of his entry as a pilgrim, Jesus caused a spectacular scene. Noticing in the colonnades the traders who were changing money or selling counters entitling their holders to the ritual lamb or doves for sacrifice, he rushed to their tables and overturned them. "Was the house of prayer to become a den of thieves?" (Matt. 22. 12–14; Mark 11. 11–17; Luke 19. 45–8). He was really blazing with the zeal of God.

It was an astonishing, mysterious day. It looks as if Jesus wanted to confront men with the truth, with their responsibilities, once and for all. When the day was over, and the western sky was red behind the three Herodian towers which crowned the wall on that side of the city, he had this further lesson for the little band of faithful followers who had stayed round him and was probably gazing at the setting sun: "I have come into this world as a light, so that all those who believe in me may continue no longer in darkness" (John 12. 46). As they returned with him to Bethany, to spend the night there, the disciples must have had much to think about.

The days which followed the astonishing Sunday of the triumphal entry were not so striking, but each of them was none the less full of significance. Jesus entered Jerusalem every day, went up to the Temple, and spoke to audiences which listened to him with enthusiasm (Luke 19. 47), while the chief priests and scribes sought means of destroying him. To Jesus, the slightest incident was an occasion for a lesson, which often took the form of a warning.

So it was all through the Monday. What precisely was the meaning of the curious episode, uncharacteristic of Christ's normally merciful manner, in which he condemned a fig-tree on which he found no figs to wither? (Matt. 21. 18, 19; Mark 11. 12–15). And who is the bad son who pretends to be submissive to his father's will, but in reality disobeys him? (Matt. 21. 28–32). Or the rebellious wine-dressers who kill their master's servants in order to seize the harvest? What is the name of the stone rejected by the builders which will be the corner-stone of the new building? (Matt. 21. 35–46; Mark 12. 1–12; Luke 20. 9–19). And do we not know these guests invited to the royal feast who refuse to attend? (Matt. 22. 1–14). One is almost afraid to understand at whom these gestures, these parables are aimed. At this moment, Israel's refusal seems to haunt Jesus' mind and to fill it with anguish.

We are hardly surprised to find that the leaders of the community sent emissaries to ask Jesus with what right he was behaving as he was. He avoided the question by himself asking them an embarrassing one (Matt. 21. 23–7; Mark 11. 27–33; Luke 20. 1–8). But we can hardly be surprised that their anger grew, and that they were on the point of laying hands on him (Luke 20. 19). Jesus cast a real challenge at his adversaries at this moment when he knew that all was to be put to the test.

The Tuesday began in the same way as the day before. Jesus went up to the Temple to speak there. Starting with a concrete fact and drawing a moral from it, as was his practice, he drew his listeners' attention to the praiseworthy action of a very poor woman who had put into the treasury an offering which was relatively big, big for her means. It is more meritorious to give from what you need than to give from plenty (Mark 12. 41–4; Luke 21. 1–4).

Suddenly the atmosphere changed. Among those present there were now listeners whose intentions were anything but friendly. Uniting to combat the prophet, the three main parties in the Jewish community had all sent their men to take the offensive against him. First it was the Herodians, whom the people accused of being too resigned to the Roman yoke because it suited their interests. They set a trap; "Is it permissible", they asked, "to pay tribute to Caesar?" How was Jesus to escape from the trap? If he answered "no", he would provoke the wrath of the occupying power; if he said "yes", that of the people. But this Galilean peasant possessed a sly wisdom which helped him out of this sort of difficulty, and he gave the famous reply, "Whose likeness is on this coin? Caesar's? Then give back to Caesar what is Caesar's, but to God what is God's" (Matt. 22. 15–22; Mark 12. 13; Luke 20. 20–6). From a skilful evasion emerged a sublime spiritual lesson.

Then the Sadducees took over the attack. They were self-righteous traditionalists who claimed that they added nothing to Moses. Above all, they did not accept the belief in the resurrection of the dead which theologians had discovered in the books of Job, Isaias and Daniel. It was on this point that they tried to put Jesus in difficulties by asking him what would happen at the resurrection to a woman who had had seven husbands; whose wife would she be? They too received a sublime spiritual lesson on the glorious lives of those who had risen from the dead, under the gaze of the God of the living (Matt. 22. 22–33; Mark 12. 18–27; Luke 30. 37–40).

Now it was the Pharisees' turn to lead the attack. They did not get very far. To ask a master like Jesus which was "the greatest commandment" was to condemn themselves to defeat in advance. It was Jesus who made them lose face by asking a precise and embarrassing question about the Messias (Matt. 22. 34–46; Mark 12. 28–37; Luke 11. 41–4). But it was a miserable pastime. One can understand why Jesus, alone with his disciples, burst out in righteous anger and gave vent to a requisitory against all these scribes, Pharisees and hypocrites, "who give their tithe of dill and cumin according to the Law, but transgress the essential part of the Law, the precept of mercy; who are like whited sepulchres, fair to look upon but full of corruption within". It was they who in days gone by killed the prophets and in days to come would crucify or exile the envoys of Christ. Never had clearer or more categorical accusations been formulated by Jesus (Matt. 23. 1–36; Mark 12. 38–40; Luke 20. 43–7).

And then the spirit of prophecy took hold of the young Messias. When it came to killing prophets, he knew what he was talking about. Repeating and enlarging the warning which he had given briefly on Sunday, he spoke again of Jerusalem

—Jerusalem which killed the prophets, which refused to understand, which would soon be deserted, abandoned (Matt. 23. 37–8; Luke 13. 34–9). As for the Temple itself, not one stone would be left on another (Matt. 24. 1, 2; Mark 13, 1, 2; Luke 21. 5, 6).

Thoroughly disturbed, the disciples asked, demanded, what would become of themselves at that time. The answer was simple and terrible. They too would be persecuted, arrested, flogged; they too would bear witness, but the Holy Spirit would have come upon them and given them the strength to endure the trial (Matt. 24. 3; Mark 23. 3–13; Luke 21. 7–19). Perhaps it was in order to tell them this that Christ called up so many terrible visions. Similarly, perhaps the only purpose in the marvellous evocation of the Last Judgement with which he concluded this inspired discourse was to repeat to the disciples the promises of future glory which he had already made by assuring them that his words would not pass away, and, above all, to remind them that, the coming of the Lord being unforeseeable, it was essential to be ready constantly to respond to his call (Matt. 24. 23–51; Mark 13. 21–37; Luke 17. 23–37 and 21), as ready as the Wise Virgins in the parable, who had oil in reserve for their lamps, or as the stewards who had to give an account of the talents entrusted to them (Matt. 6. 1–30).

But the day was not to end with these stern lessons. A saying recorded by St Matthew ends on a more consoling note, that of Christ's mercy. On the day of judgement the Lord will take account of the charity shown to the humblest, of a glass given to the thirsty. For Christ is present in all earthly suffering (Matt. 25. 34–46).

On the Wednesday Christ did not go up to Jerusalem, but stayed at Bethany with the family which sheltered him. The evangelists do not record any event or speech on this day, except for St Matthew, who locates here the anointing by Mary. Perhaps on the eve of the day which was to decide everything for him, Christ wished to devote his last hours of peace to prayer and the affection of his followers. This momentary effacement of Christ has a curious consequence; it concentrates the narrators' attention on another spectacle, that of Jesus' enemies seeking the means to destroy him and finding assistance among his followers.

At this very time, the chief priests and the elders of the people gathered in the court of the high priest, whose name was Caiphas; and there they plotted to bring Jesus into their power by cunning, and put him to death. Yet they still said, Not on the day of the feast, or perhaps there will be an uproar among the people. At that moment the spirit of evil took hold of Judas, one of the twelve, who was called Iscariot. He went to the chief priests and asked them, What will you pay me for handing him over to you? Whereupon they laid down thirty pieces of silver, and arranged to arrest Jesus when he was far from the crowd (Matt. 26. 3–6; Mark 14. 1–12; Luke 22. 2–6).

This ignoble betrayal had also been predicted. "Why, the very man I trusted most," says the Psalmist, "my own intimate friend, who shared my bread, has lifted his heel to trip me up" (Ps. 40. 10). Nevertheless, it causes as much surprise as anger. Nothing could be more mysterious than the character of this Judas who must bear the opprobrium for this infamous deed, and nothing less clear than the reasons for his action. Was it the sordid attraction of the money? But he had less need than anyone to betray his Master for the tiny sum of thirty silver *denarii*, for it was he who kept the little band's common purse. Was it irritation at seeing this disappointing Messias do nothing to ensure the triumph of his cause on the human plane? Yet his attitude after the catastrophe, his remorse, his suicide were to show that he was anything but a vulgar careerist. The truth is that Judas is unfathomable, like sin, and like the complicity with evil of every man born of flesh since Adam. His rôle would seem incomprehensible did he, too, not form part of the providential plan of Salvation through blood.

CHAPTER XVI

THE LAST SUPPER

For the Jews, celebration of the Passover was absolutely obligatory. No one could avoid it. So important was it considered that if the poor had no money to buy what was needed for the feast they were entitled to demand it from the community. During the Thursday, the disciples asked Jesus where he intended to celebrate the ritual meal. He gave them a very strange answer. Two of them, Peter and John, were to go into the city. There they would meet a man carrying a jar of water. This was not such an ordinary sight as one might think, for drawing water was a woman's task. They were to follow him to a house. They were to warn the owner of the house of his arrival, so that he could put at their disposal a big upper room furnished with carpets. There they were to make the necessary preparations (Matt. 26. 18, 19; Mark 14. 13; Luke 22. 7–19). Here again the power of the Holy Spirit was obviously at work.

This "large upper room" was probably one of those huge rooms which, in wealthy houses, occupied more or less all the first floor. It was kept for passing guests and usually an outside staircase led up to it. An ancient tradition places the scene of the Last Supper in the south-west part of the upper city, not very far from the palace of the high priests. The ceremony began when night fell, at about half-past five in the evening, that is, at the moment when, according to the Jewish way of counting the days, the 14 Nisan began.

The whole ritual was carefully prescribed. The tractate of

the Talmud entitled *Pesahim* records all the details. During
the afternoon one went to the Temple to buy the lamb without
fault or blemish required by the Law and presented it to the
sacrificers. A blast on the trumpet gave the signal for each
sacrifice. The entrails and the fat were burnt; the flesh was
taken back to the paschal house. There it was roasted, not
boiled. No bone was to be broken. One began by dipping
unleavened bread in a red sauce known as *hazareth*, at the
same time reciting a psalm and drinking a cup of wine. Then
the lamb was eaten with a sauce of "bitter herbs", that is,
horse-radish, bay, thyme, marjoram and basil. Two other cups
followed, passed from hand to hand; the third, a solemn one,
known as "the cup of benediction", marked the beginning of
the *Hallel,* the singing of Psalms 114 to 117, which exalt the
glory of the One True God. All this took place in an atmosphere of mystical joy; everyone present had to feel that he
was participating in the deliverance of Israel. "The *Hallel*",
says the Talmud, "should shatter the roof of the house!"

However, this last paschal meal with their Master was to
leave in the Apostles' minds a memory more disquieting than
joyful. From the start, Jesus had told them that it would be
the last he would eat with them before the eternal pasch in
Heaven (Luke 22. 14–16). He had added a most unexpected
ceremony to the prescribed ritual by bending down himself to
wash the feet of each of them, one after the other, in spite of
the warm protestation made on behalf of all by Simon Peter.
Christ's purpose had been—he had said so expressly—to remind them all that they were to regard themselves as the
humblest (John 13. 8–16), that, unlike earthly ambitions, their
only desire should be to resemble "the last", "him who
serves". Was this, then, the kingdom in which he would
receive them at his table, in which, sitting on thrones, they
would judge the twelve tribes of Israel? (Luke 22. 24–9; Matt.
20. 25; Mark 10. 42). They had entered straight into the mystery, a mystery which they were still far from understanding.

Then there had been the incident of Judas. On two occasions Christ had alluded to one of them, one of the Twelve, in a very disquieting manner. Who was this man "who was not clean" (John 13. 10, 11), this man referred to in the psalmist's prophetic verse, "The man who shared my bread has lifted his heel to trip me up"? (John 13. 18). To be blunt, since the word had been used, who was to betray the Master? They were all so upset that Peter made a sign to John, who, being on Jesus' left, ready to lie back on his breast, was in a position to question him. Besides, it was clear that Christ had a great affection for him and would not refuse to answer.

Jesus did in fact reply. Discreetly, as if to spare the feelings of him on whom the suspicion lay, he said, "It is the man to whom I give this piece of bread which I am dipping in the dish" (John 13. 23–6). We know now from the "Dead Sea Scrolls" that among the Essenes the first mouthful of bread dipped in wine had a precise religious significance. It was to Judas Iscariot that Jesus offered it.

The traitor may have guessed Jesus' intention and that this gesture marked him out; at any rate, he rose. The others thought that it was to attend to one of his duties as keeper of the common purse. At that point Jesus could have denounced him before the others, but he confined himself to saying, with a simplicity more moving than any show of anger, "Be quick on thy errand". Judas realized that Jesus had seen through him. He left the room; "hastily" says St John, whose whole account is clearly that of an eye-witness, the unforgettable memory of the scene. When the door opened, the evangelist notes again, "it was night" (John 13. 27–30), and the detail forms a sort of signature to the passage; so vivid and clear was it all still in his memory nearly seventy years later.

The liturgical meal pursued its course. But when the moment for the third cup came, the cup of benediction, Jesus made another innovation. The supper that these faithful Jews were all eating together commemorated one of the decisive episodes in the history of God's ancient Covenant with their people. Jesus chose this moment, that of a sacrificial rite, to affirm the new Covenant which he had come to establish; for what he was going to found was itself another sacrificial rite.

"Taking bread, blessing it and giving thanks, he broke it and gave it to his disciples, saying, Take, eat, this is my body, which will be delivered up for you. Then he took a cup, and offered thanks, and gave it to them, saying, Drink, all of you, of this; for this is my blood, of the new testament, shed for many, to the remission of sins. Do this in memory of me" (Luke 21. 19, 20; Matt. 26. 26–8; Mark 14. 22–4; cf. 1 Cor. 11. 23–5).

The custom of blessing the food and wine which one was going to eat was quite usual—and even sanctioned by the Law—in Israel. It was prescribed categorically in the Essene rule as the task of the leader of the community. What was unusual was the double formula with which Jesus accompanied it, a formula which was anything but an ordinary benediction. One wonders if the Apostles remembered at that moment that two years earlier, when they were in Galilee, their Master had declared: "I am the bread of life. . . . If anyone eats of this bread, he will live for ever, and the bread that I shall give is my own flesh, for the salvation of the world." St John was to record this whole discourse in his gospel. But the words which they had just heard were much more precise, much more mysterious. Did they understand them?

They certainly did not understand them completely; but then who can boast that he does understand these words of Christ? In the Mass, at the moment when the priest repeats them to consecrate the bread and wine, the Church has inserted two words which say everything; *mysterium fidei*. What is certain is that these simple men round Jesus, these Galilean fishermen, cannot have been in a position to interpret the words which they heard in a metaphorical or symbolical way; they would have been much more inclined to associate them with the sacrifice of the lamb which had just been consumed. That is what is taught by the Catholic Church—and by the Orthodox Churches of the East as well—namely, that in the bread and wine changed into flesh and blood the living God is really present, that it is really Christ that one absorbs when the rite is reproduced in the sacrament of the Eucharist, that we are not called simply to imitate Jesus morally, but to share in his life and, through him, in the divine life.

A divine life which transcends the limits of earthly life but goes on in eternity. St Paul says the same thing, in allusive form, in his letter to the Christians of Corinth: "Each time you eat of this bread and drink of this wine, you proclaim the death of the Lord, until he comes. . . ."

The meal was over, but it was the custom of the Jews, as of àll Orientals, to remain a long time at the table and to pursue the conversation late into the night. So it was at this Last Supper: Jesus spoke for a long time, as if he wished, at this supreme moment, to remind his followers of all that he had said to them and all that he had to say to them. We have been given a very clear picture of this last conversation by St John, who devotes nearly five chapters of his gospel to it (13. 31 to 18. 26) and reports it in a rhythmical, balanced prose of rare beauty.

The conversation began in the familiar, tender fashion, with Christ saying: "It is only for a short time that I am with you, my children." The eleven questioned him about the meaning of what he had done and what he had said. The generous Peter exclaimed, "With you, Lord, I am ready to go to prison and to death", a statement which brought a reply in which kindness and sadness were tinged with irony: "Thou art ready to lay down thy life for my sake? Believe me, by cock-crow thou wilt thrice disown me." The Apostles did not yet know, they had not yet understood. They were still at the stage of asking for tangible signs, for precise details of the road of which he spoke and which he was going to take.

But gradually the tone grew more sublime, and Jesus sketched again in outline the essentials of the message which he had brought to the world. First, he said that this message came from God, that he himself was the interpreter of the

word of God. "I am the Way, the Truth and the Life; no one
can come to the Father except through me. . . . I am the vine;
if a man lives on in me, and I in him, then he will yield
abundant fruit." "Believe me when I tell you that I am in the
Father, and the Father is in me. . . . In truth, I tell you, all
that you ask of the Father in my name he will give you."
What was this truth which he had been commissioned to bring
to the world? It can be summed up in one sentence: "Love
one another as I have loved you." That is Christ's supreme
message.

Once again the tone changed, and this time grew tenser.
Jesus drew the attention of his followers to the event that was
now near. From his lips fell words which seemed contradictory. At one moment he spoke of triumph: "Courage, I
have conquered the world! I leave you my peace, I give you
my peace"; "God has been glorified in the Son of Man; soon
he will exalt him in his own glory." At the next, sinister predictions would recur. "The hour of the Prince of this world
approaches. . . . I am leaving the world; I am returning to my
Father." Then came general prophecies about the fate which
awaited all his faithful followers: "The time is coming when
anyone who puts you to death will think that he is performing
an act agreeable to God." What did all this mean? They would
understand one day. One day St Paul would draw out a whole
splendid doctrine from these enigmatic words, the doctrine
that the death of Christ was indispensable for the salvation
of the world, that by offering himself as a victim he gained
the divine pardon for the huge mass of sinners. His death
would have a meaning, like that of the sacrificed lamb which
caused the children of Israel to be spared. "This is the greatest
love that a man can show, that he should lay down his life for
his friends."

Jesus concluded this unique evening with some admirably
inspired words, which form the most beautiful prayer ever
uttered. He asked the Father to take pity on the men whom he
entrusted to him, on all those who believed in him and fol-

lowed his lessons: "I pray that they may all be one ... that they should all be one, as we are one; that while thou art in me, I may be in them for ever."

No doubt it was too late to return to Bethany. After descending the slope of Mount Sion by a stepped road, which archaeologists have uncovered, they crossed the Cedron, then swollen and muddy, and stopped in a friendly paddock, planted with olive trees, where they had often been before. It was called Gethsemani, the "oil-press". They meant to spend the night there wrapped in their cloaks, a common thing for pilgrims to do. It was this spot that witnessed one of the most shattering scenes in the life of Jesus Christ, the scene that was to put the seal on the sacrificial vocation to which the institution of the Eucharist had just given sacramental expression. Since, according to the evangelists' own admissions, none of the Apostles witnessed the scene, and since afterwards Jesus had neither the time nor the opportunity to describe it to them, people have wondered how it could be known with the accuracy with which it is related in the Bible. There is a theory, resting on a very ancient tradition, which may provide an explanation. St Mark the evangelist records a little further on (14. 51) that at the moment when Jesus was arrested a young man tried to follow the troop which took him away. Pursued by the guards, he fled, naked, leaving in their hands the linen shirt which he was wearing. The detail is so precise that it looks as if it is an auto-biographical one. According to the theory mentioned above, Mark was the son of the owner of the house in which the Last Supper was held; he followed Jesus and his disciples clandestinely to the olive garden, hid behind the trunk of an old tree, and thus saw and heard everything.

"Sit down here", said Jesus to his disciples, "while I go a little further and pray. You pray too, so that you do not yield to temptation." He took with him only Peter, James and John. Fear and horror, grief and anguish were beginning to rise in his heart. "My soul is sad unto death," he said. "Abide here and keep watch with me." He himself went off and, prostrating himself on the ground, prayed: "Father, if it is possible, and to you everything is possible, take away this chalice from before me! But thy will be done, not mine." Returning to the three disciples, he found them asleep. "So you cannot watch for one hour with me," he said. "The spirit is willing, but the flesh is weak." Going off alone again, he repeated: "Father, if this chalice may not pass me by, but I must drink it, then thy will be done." By now he was in an agony of anguish; sweat glistened on his face and fell to the ground like thick drops of blood (Matt. 26; Mark 14; Luke 22).

It was a terrible but splendid moment. Humanly speaking, there is something tremendously consoling about it: if God incarnate went through this trial, we can all, everyone of us, recognize ourselves in him. Many saints are reported to have known similar trials; St Teresa of Lisieux, for example, devoured by doubt, fascinated by the void, only a few hours before the supreme sacrifice. At that moment Jesus identified himself with man to the point where the process becomes a mystery; he identified himself with sinful man terrified by the approach of death and judgement, he saw, in all its truth and horror, nature wounded by evil. But, in the last analysis, the situation remained what it had been when he met the same temptation earlier on and made an act of submission and of confidence in the divine wisdom, the only act in which man can find comfort and consolation. The great anguish had been conquered, the temptation to use the divine power to spoil God's plan had been surmounted, and the *"fiat voluntas tua"* had been uttered; there was nothing left for the Son of Man to do but to allow the consummation of the sacrifice which he had come to accomplish on earth. The hour had struck.

CHAPTER XVII

THE HOUR OF THE

POWER OF DARKNESS

The events of Thursday night and Friday morning have been related by the four evangelists (Matt. 26. 27; Mark 14. 15; Luke 22. 23; John 18. 19) with extraordinary simplicity and persuasive force. One feels that when they wrote years afterwards these men were still so impressed by the events that they found it impossible not to give a concrete, direct account without any commentary. Not once did the idea occur to them that Christ could have employed supernatural forces to balance the terrible coalition at work against him. They all show him resigned, delivered up to wickedness, truly offered like a victim; more poignant—and more disquieting—in this attitude than an accused man who struggles and counter-attacks. It is all purely, dreadfully human.

A band of men came down the stepped path. There was the rattle of arms, the glow of torches and lanterns. The band consisted of servants, Temple guards, a few scribes, and perhaps some Roman auxiliary troops to keep order. They arrived in the garden of olive trees. Jesus was there all right, with only a very small group of his closest followers; the arrest would be easy; the traitor had done his work well. Judas went up to Jesus, greeted him, and kissed him—on the hand, no doubt, as disciples of a rabbi were accustomed to do. One sad remark escaped Jesus: "Judas, wouldst thou betray the Son of Man with a kiss?" Then he walked towards the constables, "Whom do you seek?" he asked. "Jesus of Nazareth," they replied. "It is I," he said, "let the others go." At that moment the impetuous Simon Peter jumped forward, his sword in his hand. Jesus stopped him with a word and surrendered to the guards, who marched him off. "Your time has come," he said, "darkness has its will." All human methods were vain; it was not by them that the power of darkness would be conquered.

Thus began what has often been called "the trial of Jesus". It was a strange trial, one in which legal rules were to be so outrageously violated that in our day honourable Jews have demanded the annulment of the unjust verdict in which it ended. For it was one of the great principles of the Mosaic Law and of Israelite jurisprudence to seek to guarantee the rights of the defendant, to do everything possible to ensure that he was not the victim of a plot. The employment of a police spy was itself forbidden by the Law in virtue of an article of Leviticus (19. 16). Cases in which a man's life was at stake had to be heard in the light of day; the Talmud contains several passages in which this is stated categorically. Similarly, it was absolutely forbidden to strike an accused man, to provoke the slightest physical resistance. Many other flagrant illegalities could be cited in connection with this trial, which was to be conducted in such a strange way, during the night, after secret meetings, more after the fashion of a plot than a normal piece of judicial business. Moreover, it ended necessarily in a sentence of death, which was quite contrary to the general tendency in Israel at that time. A rabbi who lived in those days said: "A Sanhedrin which had eleven men executed in seventy years would seem a destructive one to me." Hatred of Christ must have been strong indeed for people to disobey both the letter of the Law and its intentions.

Jesus was taken first to Annas. Why Annas? As far as we can see, because he was the mainspring of the whole affair. A former high priest himself, head of a priestly family seven members of which were to attain the mitre and pectoral, he was an influential person. Renan calls him "the real author of this terrible drama". Yet it does not seem from the gospels that it was he who conducted the decisive conversation with Jesus. No doubt it was enough for this man, who could distinguish real power from the appearance of it, to have seen his opponent before him, at his mercy.

The trial proper began before Caiphas, the reigning High Priest, a vain, ambitious mediocrity, servile enough before the Romans to keep his position for eighteen years. At the news of the arrest, scribes, Elders of the People and Doctors of the Law hastened to the palace of the high priests; it was not a regularly convoked Sanhedrin, but rather a sort of tribunal of the people, with all the sinister overtones the phrase implies. However, there were enough people present for the Sanhedrin to endorse its decision automatically.

The interrogation began. It dealt with Jesus' teaching and his disciples. Jesus was astonished. Had he ever spoken secretly? Spies could have heard him in the Temple court. No matter; witnesses were produced. They had heard him boast of destroying the Temple; Jesus had in fact said, by way of a parable, "Destroy this temple and I will build it up again in three days" (John 2. 19). But in any case the accusation was so clumsy that it misfired. Then Caiphas went straight to the essential point; he put the question of questions, "Art thou the Christ, the Son of the blessed God?" In Jesus' eyes, Caiphas, worthless as he may have been in himself, represented the authority of his people, and Jesus did not attempt to evade the question. His reply was categorical: "I am. And one day you will see the Son of Man sitting at the right hand of God's power. . . ." To call oneself God, to make oneself God, was certainly blasphemy for a man. Caiphas could well tear his garments, as he was bound to when he heard a blasphemy. If Jesus had only called himself the Messias, there would have been room for discussion, but to call oneself the Son of God was a crime. What need was there of witnesses or supplementary questions? The guards were ordered to take him away; the Sanhedrin would decide his fate.

When Jesus emerged into the courtyard of the Palace, an incident had just occurred which puts the finishing touch to his isolation and abandonment. Peter, who had followed him at a distance, had entered the courtyard of the High Priest, on the watch for news. As it was a cold night he had gone up to the brazier lit by the guards. A maidservant had recognized him, pointed him out and denounced him. Peter, terrified, had sworn that he did not belong to the Galilean's band, that he did not know the individual, that he had no acquaintance with him. He had just sworn for the third time when Jesus appeared, looked at him—and the cock crew. All Peter could do was flee into the night, weeping.

Jesus remained alone, more alone than ever. The servants and soldiery had him at their mercy. They decided to see what he was capable of, this prophet, this magician, this sorcerer, this self-styled Messias. They played a very amusing game; they blindfolded him, struck him hard, and asked amid laughter, "Come on, Messias, guess who struck you! A prophet should be able to guess where the blows came from!" The scene was a painful one; prisons in all ages have witnessed similar, and worse, ones. Jesus replied to all these insults with silence. To follow Christ, says the Epistle to the Hebrews, one must bear "the ignominy he bore" (13. 13). And one must also share his heroic acceptance.

In the first light of day the Sanhedrin met, probably in the Temple, perhaps even in the "hall of hewn stone" reserved for it, the *Liscal Haggasith,* one of whose doors opened on to sacred ground, the other on to profane ground. The former was for the judges, the latter for the accused, in accordance with the Law. A case could only be judged if the High Priest had carried out an investigation previously. Conversations in the night could hardly be regarded as a proper investigation! There had to be an accuser, who was solemnly reminded that he was taking on himself the responsibility for a man's life and that calumnious denunciations were visited with terrible punishments. Finally, so that the judges should not be carried away by passion, a sentence could only be carried out after an interval of twenty-four hours, during which period any judge had the right to change his opinion, but only to the advantage of the defendant. The power of darkness was certainly at work; which of these wise precautions was to be observed in the case of Jesus?

Even St Luke, whose account is the most precise at this point, gives the impression of a rigged session. The question already posed by Caiphas was repeated in a different form. Thinking no doubt that his affirmation did not allow room for discussion, Jesus answered at first in ironical terms. Then, changing his mind, he repeated almost word for word what he had said to the High Priest: "The Son of God? Yes, I am." To which the Council replied, in a voice that one might have hoped would have been less unanimous, "The case is over! What need have we of witnesses? We have heard the blasphemy with our own ears!"

Blasphemy was the greatest of all crimes, the one which in any circumstances deserved death. So the sentence which the Sanhedrin would have liked to pass was death. I say "would have liked to" advisedly, for it could not. We read in the tractate of the Talmud entitled *Sanhedrin* (1. 1, 7, 2): "Forty years before the destruction of the Temple Israel was deprived of the power to judge cases in which a man's life was at stake." The Temple was destroyed in A.D. 70, so the Jews' loss of the right to have criminals put to death dated from somewhere about the very year in which Jesus died. The attitude of the Jewish authorities and subsequently that of Pilate prove clearly that in fact the Sanhedrin was not free.

So the matter had to be explained to the procurator. But, to a Roman, to condemn a man to death because he said he was "the Son of God" would be completely ridiculous. Other charges had to be discovered. That was not difficult. The teaching of the self-styled Messias was full of scandalous sayings which it would be easy to exploit against him. He had proclaimed himself King. He had declared that it was not necessary to pay tribute to the Romans. And besides he was causing a commotion among the people that might become serious. Was that not sufficient to send him to "hang on the wood"?

No doubt news of the Sanhedrin's verdict soon spread through the city. One of the men who heard it was cut to the heart by it. This was the man who had been the instrument of hatred: Judas. Here again, the mystery of this man's psychology thickens. Had he not weighed the consequences of his action? What he did now seems absurd, incomprehensible. He rushed to the Council and threw down on the ground the accursed money, the thirty pieces of silver which he had been paid for his treachery. It was too late. "What is that to us?" they replied with a shrug of the shoulders. All he could do was flee, pursued by a remorse so great that any appeal to the divine mercy seemed out of the question. There was nothing left for him to do but kill himself (Matt. 27. 3–10; Acts 1. 16–20).

"It was dawn," says St John; 5.52 a.m., to be precise. The members of the Great Council had gone to the fortress of Antonia, where the procurator resided when he came up from Caesarea to Jerusalem to keep an eye on the pilgrimages. They were probably escorted by a fair number of inquisitive people. They took care not to enter; to go into the house of a Gentile was to make oneself unclean, and none of these pious persons wished to soil himself right in the middle of the Passover. So a dialogue began in rather curious circumstances. The Roman, who had been hastily awoken, stood leaning on the balustrade which ran round the top of the fortress wall; the Jews were massed beneath him, shouting excitedly. As for Jesus, he was brought in and stood in the paved court where, St John tells us, Pilate had set up his praetorium (19. 13).

Archaeology here provides a detail which cannot but move those who believe in Jesus. After the capture of Jerusalem the

Antonia was razed to the ground, like the whole Temple hill; on the site a pagan temple was built, which was later to yield in turn to the mosque of Omar. But excavations among the remains of the Roman buildings have disclosed the paving stones of Pilate's praetorium. One can see these enormous slabs—six feet six inches by five feet, and eighteen inches thick—in the basement of the convent of the Ladies of Sion, slabs which were trodden by the feet of Christ.

"What is your charge against this man?" asked Pilate. The members of the Council did not dare to reply directly. "Have him executed," they said evasively. "If he were not a criminal, we should not have brought him to you." As he insisted, they reeled off the agreed charges; this Roman had to understand that he was confronted with someone who had preached sedition.

In the end, everything was going to depend on Pilate. What sort of a man was he? He is well known to history, through Tacitus, Josephus and Philo. In 1961 an inscription bearing his name was discovered at Caesarea; it was on a monument in honour of Tiberius.[1] What we know of his career and of his psychology suggests that he was a very average administrator whose only concern was to avoid trouble. The Jews accused him of being heavy-handed; in any case, he distrusted them. So he questioned Jesus himself.

"Is it true that thou art the King of the Jews?" he asked. Jesus replied, "My kingdom is not of this world. . . ." Pilate did not understand very clearly. "Thou art a king, then?" "Yes, thou hast said it. I am a king. I came into the world to bear witness to the truth, and whoever serves the truth belongs to me." For the Roman, the case was over; this was one of these inoffensive dreamers who said that they were in search of the Truth. What was Truth?

[1] Curiously enough, in this inscription Pontius Pilate is described as "Prefect of Judaea", not "Procurator". It seems that in the early days of the empire there was a prefect in Judaea.

But the pack which led the attack against Jesus would not listen to him. If Pilate said "I find nothing criminal in this man", the only reply he received was a tumult of shouting. On the pretext that Jesus was a Galilean, he tried to get rid of the affair by handing it over to Herod Antipas, the tetrarch of Galilee, who happened to be in Jerusalem for the Passover; but the attempt was vain; "the fox" was too cunning to take on an awkward case like this. Pilate had to make up his mind. His embarrassment was growing; he felt clearly that an attempt was being made to manipulate him. His wife, who believed in dreams, had just warned him that she was worried by a dream; it was essential that he should not get mixed up in this affair at any price. But how could he help it? Every idea of Pilate's failed. It was the custom at the Passover to pardon a man condemned to death; did they not wish him to pardon Jesus, who had done nothing serious? Appropriately drilled, the crowd shrieked back: "No, no! Barabbas, pardon Barabbas! He is an ordinary bandit. He at least did not call himself 'the Son of God'!"

At this point Pilate's conduct became rather strange. Perhaps because Jesus had in fact disturbed public order or else because he wished to give the crowd some kind of satisfaction, he ordered that Jesus should be flogged. The order was carried out; it was a terrible punishment. Tied by the hands to a short stake, the condemned man received forty blows—less one, said the Jewish Law—on his back from a sort of knout of thongs loaded with tiny lumps of metal or small pieces of sheep's bone. When the man was pulled up again, he was dripping with blood and tottering. It was this human wreck that the soldiers, taking advantage no doubt of Pilate's absence, mocked and taunted. They decked him out in a red military cloak, put a derisory reed sceptre in his hand and stuck on his head a crown made of the branches of a shrub with long thorns.

The sight was such a painful one that Pilate, returning to the praetorium, was moved by pity. "Here is the man!" he shouted to the crowd. His intention is clear; did they not think that this was enough, that he had been sufficiently punished? But the fever rose again and the crowd became frantic. It had its prey and it wanted to kill. The Roman repeated, "I find no fault in this man"; the crowd growled back, "He proclaimed himself king! If you release him you betray Caesar's trust!" This time the argument struck home. Pilate knew that the people he ruled could easily denounce him to the Emperor. So much the worse for this poor wretch! And the scene ended with the crowd shrieking savagely, "Crucify him! Crucify him!"

CHAPTER XVIII

THE GUILT OF BLOOD

It was all over. Jesus was finished, delivered up to his enemies. Nothing could now prevent the drama reaching its dreadful conclusion, the one prophesied by Christ himself, "the lifting up" on the Cross. At this point, when we are about to see the greatest crime in history committed, the supreme iniquity, the symbol and image of so much that goes on around us, there is one tormenting question that we cannot help asking: who was responsible? Who bore the responsibility for shedding the blood of this just man?

The Christian tradition gives two contradictory answers. In the Creed the shame is borne by Pontius Pilate, who alone is named in connection with Christ's passion: "suffered under Pontius Pilate...." It is certainly true that, from a legal point of view, the Procurator of Judaea must bear the responsibility for this judicial murder. It was in his power to release an accused man whom he had acknowledged to be innocent. He did not do so, and we know how human—only too human— his reasons were. One feels inclined to leave this civil servant alone with his own conscience.

But even if cowardice and weakness of character are not valid excuses, surely the moral responsibility falls still more heavily on those who exploited these wretched faults to attain their ignoble ends? We have only to read the gospels to realize that Pilate, proud Roman though he may have been, was in the hands of his subjects. Threatened with the possibility of being denounced in a more or less slanderous fashion to Tiberius, could he do anything but yield? The neurasthenic hermit of Capri was not given to joking in matters of this sort. That is what many Christian writers have thought ever since the time of the Fathers of the Church. "Pilate shared in their crimes to the extent of his actions," says St Augustine, "but, compared with them, he seems much less guilty."

"Compared with them"; who were "they"? If we open the Fourth Gospel we shall find the answer. It is "the Jews" who are the leaders in the whole affair, right down to the terrible cry of "Put him to death! Crucify him!" Similarly, in the Acts of the Apostles (2. 23), when St Peter addresses the "men of Israel", he reproaches them with having "crucified, put to death at the hands of the executioners", Jesus of Nazareth. What is still more convincing is that it is the Jew St Paul, a former disciple of the rabbis of Israel, who writes, as a self-evident truth, "The Jews . . . killed the Lord Jesus" (1 Thess. 2. 15). So it is the Jews collectively, the Jewish people as a whole, that the written evidence seems to arraign.

Deicides! The accusation has been continually repeated right down the ages and has undoubtedly provided the intellectual vice known as Anti-Semitism with one of its apparent justifications. The tradition is so well established that it is extremely difficult for a Christian—whether he be Catholic, Orthodox or Protestant—to realize that the statement "the Jews crucified Jesus" raises some very difficult questions.[1]

Did all the Jews in Palestine—quite apart from those dispersed throughout the Empire—know Jesus? It is extremely doubtful whether they did. The main part of his mission took place in Galilee, a remote province of which the pious Jews of Jerusalem thought little. How big were the "crowds" which followed Jesus? The biggest gatherings known, those for which the loaves were multiplied, did not amount to more than five thousand people; that is a large number, but it is

[1] This chapter repeats, from a fresh angle, what the author wrote in 1944 in the first editions of *Jesus in his Time*.

not a whole people. In spite of short trips to Judaea, Jesus was certainly not very well known in that region; the proof of this is provided by St Matthew, who says in his account of Jesus' solemn entry into Jerusalem—the one on "Palm Sunday"—that the spectators asked each other, "Who is it?" Besides, St John says that "Jesus often hid himself." Of the one million people—at the outside—who lived in the Holy Land at that time, did 50,000 know who Jesus of Nazareth was?

And among these, can we say that opposition to the person and message of Jesus was general? In other words, were "all the Jews" against him? If we answer "Yes", then that means that we have decided to disregard the constant evidence of the Gospel. It means forgetting the admirable men—all of them Jews—who in response to Christ's call left their nets or their custom-house table to follow him for ever. It means forgetting the admirable women who voluntarily made themselves the little band's servants; Martha and Mary of Bethany, and the repentant sinner who poured ointment on his bare feet. It means forgetting the masses—St Luke says "all the people" (19. 48)—who hastened to hear him, the "multitude smitten with admiration" mentioned by St Mark (11. 18). There is nothing implausible or imaginary about these statements. The words which St John attributes to Jesus' opponents, "If we let him carry on like this, everyone will believe in him" (11. 48), were more than likely a just assessment of the situation.

Moreover, did the average Jew actually possess the reasons which he might have considered valid for condemning Jesus? In the last analysis, the tragic dispute between Jesus and "the leaders of the Jewish people", the chief priests and theologians, concerned his messianic status. If he really was the Messias, everyone ought to have bowed to him; so he was not, he could not be. But what did "the people" as a whole know about it? Jesus himself said very seldom that he was the Messias. He said so explicitly only once, to the Samaritan woman, an unimportant foreigner. As for his disciples, every time that his divine, transcendent character was manifested —at the Transfiguration, for example—he imposed silence on them. And we have already seen that the miracles he performed were not in themselves, in the eyes of the Jews of his age, proofs of his messianic nature, and still less of his divinity, since ordinary prophets had done as much.

So to say, "The Jews knew Jesus, and they refused to regard him as the Messias," is to make a gratuitous assertion in obvious contradiction with the written evidence and the facts.

Does it follow that the Jews bear no responsibility at all in "the business of Jesus"? Certainly not. That is why, in certain Jewish circles, there has been a campaign to circumscribe this responsibility and to acquit the people of Israel as a whole. "The Jews of today", says one of them, Enelow, "deplore the tragic death of Jesus." In 1933 a Jewish "tribunal", sitting at Jerusalem, is even supposed to have "rehabilitated" Jesus.[2] Good. But who, then, among the Jewish people, took the initiative in organizing the scandalous "trial"? Who arranged this piece of wickedness for reasons that were a mixture of high politics and sordid personal interest?

The answer is provided by numerous passages in the New Testament. St James formulates it, in cutting terms, in his epistle: "It is you, men of riches, who have condemned and murdered the Just One!" (5. 1–6). And St James is depicted as a pious Jew, a strict observer of the Law of Moses. The authors of the three synoptic gospels categorically accuse "the high priests, the leaders of the people, the elders, the scribes, the doctors of the Law", all those whom St Paul calls "the rulers of this world" (1 Cor. 2. 8). This comes down to incriminating the governing class, the politicians and the intellectuals, the well-to-do and the self-righteous. These people could keep abreast of the mission conducted by the

---

[2] This is the subject of Diego Fabbri's play, *The Case against Jesus*.

young Galilean prophet; they could realize the threat to the established order implied in his message; they had the means of setting in motion the judicial machinery, including that of the Roman occupying power.

To be honest, we must acknowledge that even in the ranks of these well-to-do people there were exceptions, men who had considerable admiration and affection for Jesus, men like Nicodemus, Joseph of Arimathea and the anonymous "rich young man". Even some of the Pharisees had had friendly relations with Jesus and had gone so far as to invite him to their houses. But these exceptions can be counted on the fingers of one hand. The truth is that it was the priestly class and the leaders of the important religious sects who organized the affair and really bear the responsibility for the shedding of blood. There was the High Priest, Annas, whom Renan regarded as "the real author of the judicial murder"; the other pontiff, the wretched Caiphas, who had expressed the opinion that it was expedient that one man should die; the Sadducee clique, so closely bound to the Romans, which feared that the "Nazarene" agitation would provoke a reaction from the occupying power; and finally the Pharisees, whose loftiest convictions, interests and pride were all injured by Jesus' teaching. From the moment that its leaders decided to oppose the self-styled Messias the people as a whole was bound to follow them.

This conclusion does not put an end to the questions. Another, just as difficult, arises. To what extent can a people be regarded as collectively responsible for a crime committed by one section of it, even if this section is the governing class? The terrible logic of history teaches us that the faults of a government are always paid for by the people; but one of the clearest lessons of history is also that peoples feel a certain solidarity with the men who bring them fame, whether they are conquering soldiers or creative geniuses. So such a thing as collective responsibility does exist, just as there is collective fame and collective pride. Moreover, there is an ingrained tendency in the human mind to admit it.[3]

Yet something inside us rebels and protests. Do all the French feel collectively responsible for the death of Joan of Arc or for the execution of Louis XVI? Do the English all feel responsible for the kings and queens who were beheaded? Or the Germans for Hitler's concentration camps and gas chambers? The Americans for the annihilation of the Indians or the miseries of segregation? Confronted with a crime committed by a group, a class, a régime or a ruler, the individual conscience instinctively reacts by protesting, "Not guilty!" Why not give the little people of Israel credit for the same reaction?

The responsibility for the death of Jesus cannot be confined to the judicial and historical plane alone, for this death is not simply a historical fact, the result of a human judgement. The only complete answer to the questions which arise on this occasion is of a supernatural order. In the economy of salvation the death of the just man Jesus was necessary; it perfected the mystery of the Incarnation. The men who decided it were surely unwitting instruments of the design.

To pass anything like a fair judgement on this perplexing problem we must try to imagine what our own attitude would have been had we lived in Jesus' time, under the rod of the priests and the pedantic zeal of the rabbis. How many of the Christians alive today, had they lived at Jerusalem in the year 30, would have been on Christ's side, and how many in the ranks of his executioners? The authorities spoke; they referred

[3] A tendency so deeply ingrained that when the Jewish historian Jules Isaac dedicated his moving book *Jesus and Israel,* which is devoted to the purpose of showing that not *all* the Jews crucified Jesus, that is, to the purpose of destroying the theory of collective responsibility, he wrote on the title page: "To my wife and daughter, martyred by the Germans, killed simply because their name was Isaac." Was it all the Germans who killed those whom Jules Isaac mourns? Were the German Christians who were beheaded for not yielding to Hitler responsible? (In the last edition of the book issued during the author's lifetime the dedication was altered.)

to great principles, the established order, the most sacred loyalties. "Do not many of us," writes Fr de Lubac in his *Drama of Atheistic Humanism,* "profess Catholicism for the same reasons of personal comfort and social conformism which, twenty centuries ago, would have impelled us to reject the disturbing novelty of the Good News?"

The final answer to the question is probably the one given by Péguy: "It was not the Jews that crucified Jesus, but the sins of all of us." As Péguy also said—it is one of his profoundest aphorisms—each one of us shares in "the universal evil of humanity", so that every time an injustice is committed each one of us bears a little of the responsibility for it. The mystery of Israel, God's people, is precisely that it is both the witness and the victim of this responsibility. It was the historical repository of a unique revelation, that of the one true God. It enjoyed the advantage of an extraordinary privilege, the Covenant with this God. By rejecting Jesus, by condemning Jesus, the leaders of the Jewish people were unwittingly faithful to the same supernatural vocation which had guided Israel's destiny right down the centuries. They represented a class of men who exist in every age and every country and who never cease to crucify Jesus.

So Jesus was judged, condemned and crucified. At this point one might think that there was no more to be said, that sinful man could only bow his head and weep. But all was not over; on the contrary, it was just beginning. For the drama of Calvary which was to form the conclusion of the sinister "trial" of Good Friday, the culmination of the Jewish leaders' terrible plot—and the punishment of our own infidelity—does not end in an abyss of darkness or the vengeance of an angry God. From the lips of Jesus, hanging there on the cross, were to fall the words which transform anguish into hope: "Father, forgive them, for they know not what they do."

Moreover, no one is excluded from this mercy, which falls like rain with the crucified man's blood, not even Annas,

Caiphas, Pilate, the Sadducees, the Pharisees or the self-righteous of every age. The people of Israel, whether it knows it or not, whether it accepts it or not, receives the benefit of it like any other people. As Péguy puts it again, "The Jews, who were only the instrument, share like the rest in the fountain of salvation."

CHAPTER XIX

"WHEN I HAVE BEEN LIFTED UP"

To the north-west, opposite the slopes of Gareb, the ramparts of Jerusalem formed a salient. This salient contained the Gate of Ephraim, which led out to Jaffa, and, a little further to the east, the Fishmarket Gate, the start of the road to the Lake of Genesareth via Samaria. As was usual in the ancient world, tombs lined the roads. It was a sinister quarter, haunted by stray dogs and vultures, for there were often things there for them to eat.

Here stood the wooden crosses on which those sentenced to capital punishment died. There was a hillock of bare lime-stone—"the bald skull" in popular parlance; *Golgotha* in Aramaic, *Calvarius* in Latin—permanently planted with poles eight feet high, to which only a cross-beam had to be added to produce a cross, the classic device for the execution of run-away slaves or criminals such as bandits and rebels.

"Put to death false prophets on great feast days," said the Law. Their death was to be public, "so that the people shall see and tremble" (Deut. 13. 11). These bodies hanging on wooden crosses would be seen by all the pilgrims arriving from Caesarea, Jaffa or Galilee; they provided a ghastly lesson. It was to this bare hillock that Jesus was taken.

The Jews had a complete ceremonial for leading a man to his death. A herald walked at the head of the procession, reminding people of the crime which had caused the arrest; theological students escorted the condemned man, exhorting him to repentance; and a representative of the Sanhedrin watched over the whole operation. We do not receive the impression that all this was done for Jesus of Nazareth; on the other hand, the procurator had the execution supervised by a centurion and a company of soldiers.

Before the procession set out, Pilate gave orders that a placard should be written out. It was another Roman custom to fix above the condemned man's head an inscription explaining the reason for his sentence. What was to be put up for Jesus? No doubt the governor had trembled inwardly when the crowd had made a clear allusion to a possible denunciation; he had his revenge by describing Jesus as "the King of the Jews". Such was the inscription that every passer-by could read in Latin, Greek and Hebrew. The mockery was clumsy, but the spiteful politicians who had accused Jesus of wanting to make himself king were hoist with their own petard. All their protests met an amused refusal.

The procession set out at the beginning of the sixth hour (John 19. 14), that is, at about half-past eleven in the morning. It left the Antonia and made its way slowly up through the stepped streets towards the ramparts. Such was the first "Way of the Cross", subsequently commemorated by pious Christians in a simple, touching liturgy with its traditional "fourteen stations".[1] Not everything in the tradition is historical; there is no solid evidence for Christ's "three falls", the meeting with his mother, or Veronica's gesture, of such symbolic beauty. This woman of the people is supposed to have wiped Jesus' battered, bleeding face with a cloth. The essential facts, as recorded by the evangelists, are poignant enough in themselves. The unhappy man, exhausted by lack of sleep and the flogging which he had received, carrying on his shoulder the heavy beam intended for his own crucifixion,

[1] Pope Paul VI followed the Way of the Cross during his pilgrimage to Jerusalem, on February 4th, 1964.

stumbling, falling, was so obviously at the end of his tether that the centurion of the guard commandeered a passer-by—a Jew from Cyrene, called Simon—to help him. The Christian pilgrims of the Middle Ages who were to follow the procession's route on their knees called it the *Via Dolorosa*, and the gate by which they thought it left the city the *Porta Dolorosa*.[2] Long years before, the prophet had foretold that the Messias offered up for the redemption of the world would be a man of sorrows (Isaias 53).

Crucifixion was not a Jewish mode of punishment. The punishments prescribed in the Bible were stoning—this was the most usual one—burning, rarely inflicted but then in circumstances more horrible than those of the medieval stake, and decapitation, the penalty paid by idolators and apostates. Crucifixion was probably Persian in origin; it was carried to the shores of the Mediterranean by the Phoenicians, adopted at Rome quite early on—by Tarquinius Superbus, so it was said—and subsequently spread everywhere. In Judaea itself the last priestly dynasty, the Hasmonaeans, had made abundant use of it. It was decidedly a shameful punishment, inflicted on criminals of lowly origin; Verres, the Proconsul of Sicily, had been vehemently attacked by Cicero for insulting Roman honour by inflicting it on a Roman citizen. Cicero calls it "a cruel and horrible punishment" in his Verrine orations. Fastened to the wood by nails or ropes, the body, dragging down on the arms, stiffened in a terrible cramp; the lungs became blocked; a fever arose, drying the mucous secretions and making the heart beat irregularly. But death could be a long time coming; as long as three days, according to Petronius. All the more so because, to prevent the flesh of the hands from tearing and the body from falling, care was taken to drive in the nails between the bones of the wrist; often a sort of crutch shaped like a rhinoceros's horn was

[2] In fact, the procession probably used the Gate of Ephraim (see the map on page 123).

placed between the legs of the condemned man; this prevented asphyxia through tetanization from occurring quickly. One can understand that a punishment of this sort was greatly feared. During the Jewish War, the defenders of one place preferred to surrender it rather than see their leader, who had been taken prisoner, crucified.

When the procession reached Golgotha, Jesus was pushed down on to the ground and fixed, with outstretched arms, to the beam which he had carried. Then some kind of tackle was used to hoist the beam up to the notch provided in the vertical stake. The suffering and horror began. They were so well known that the Law (cf. Proverbs 31. 6) prescribed that the condemned man should be given a "strong liquor" to drink, probably with some kind of hypnotic effect to induce a certain degree of insensibility. There was a guild of women at Jerusalem which undertook this supreme act of charity. But when Jesus was offered "wine mixed with myrrh", he refused it. He would not cheat death (Mark 15. 23).

All that then remained to do was wait. Two thieves had been crucified at the same time as Jesus. Slowly the inquisitive people who had followed the procession dispersed. At the foot of the Cross there remained only a small knot of Jesus' faithful followers: his mother, Mary Magdalen, a few other brave women and one single disciple, John; all the others had fled in dismay and gone into hiding in the poorer quarter of the city. There was also the squad of four guards responsible for keeping watch right to the end. Traditionally, the clothes of the condemned man were left to those who had participated in the execution; the usage was to be codified in the Digest. So the soldiers divided the garments into four and shared them out among themselves. However, as Jesus' tunic was a good one, without seams, they decided not to cut it up but to draw lots for it. They could hardly have known that in doing this they were fulfilling a prophecy (Ps. 21. 19). So true was it that these dreadful events formed part of a more than human plan.

Death took three hours to do its work; three hours of sufferings so dreadful that no words could describe them. There was physical suffering, of course, as we have just seen, but there was also mental suffering, and this was even greater: the suffering of the just victim of iniquity, the suffering of the messenger of love crucified by hatred, a hatred which was not disarmed even by the sight of this pitiful, tortured body. Passers-by and loiterers taunted the dying man: "Come now," they said, "thou who wouldst destroy the temple and build it up in three days, rescue thyself; come down from that cross!" One can almost hear them. And the soldiers, probably Bedouins or Samaritans, chimed in too: "If thou art the king of the Jews, save thyself!" (Matt. 27. 40; Mark 15. 29; Luke 23. 37).

Yet Jesus' only response to this abject behaviour consisted of words of mercy. He heard the mocking, and murmured, "Father, forgive them, for they know not what they do." This comforting sentence wipes out at one stroke the crowd's savage shout to Pilate, "Let his blood be upon us!" It is so comforting that a sinner cannot hear it without feeling a thrill of hope. To one of the thieves crucified at his side—the other joined in the dreadful taunts of the bystanders—Jesus spoke with the same infinite tenderness, promising him forgiveness, salvation, a share in the Kingdom (Luke 23. 39–41). At the very moment when it was accomplished, the sacrifice of God Incarnate spreads out in grace over the earth; was it not also for each of those who had condemned, tortured and insulted him that he was shedding his blood?

All this transcended earthly prospects. The sacrificial death of this just man was a supernatural necessity—*sine sanguine non fit remissio*—but it was none the less a scandal, an attack on world order. That is why the physical world itself reacted, testifying to its horror: "from the sixth to the ninth hour there was darkness over the earth", say the synoptic gospels. So it had been foretold by the old prophet Amos (8. 9). There was an atmosphere of anguish and terror, under a black sky, in the breath of the *Khamsin* from Arabia, in which the most familiar objects assume a sinister, frightening look and one has the sensation of breathing in death and abandonment. *"Eli, Eli, lamma sabachthani!"* (Matt. 27. 46). From the lips of the man on the cross came these Aramaic words, which translate the beginning of Psalm 21, the great prophetic psalm: "My God, my God, why hast thou forsaken me?" All was said; these were almost Jesus' last words on earth, as if to show men that Christ himself had taken on himself their great fear of death, their boundless distress.

A few moments earlier, he had touchingly asked John, the beloved disciple, to take care of his mother. Then, in very human and humble fashion, he had begged for a drink. And by the ninth hour all was over.

It is St John (19), the only one of the evangelists to have been an eye-witness of the drama, who describes the supreme moment. Jesus had nothing more to say to the earth; the last words he uttered, words overcoming the anguish of abandonment, were directed to his Father: "Father, into thy hands I commend my spirit." They formed a last act of faith, and were to be put by the Church into the mouths of the dying, so that they could draw hope from them.

The Synoptics for their part report that wonders marked the moment when Christ's divine soul left the human flesh which he had voluntarily put on to suffer and to die. Was there an earthquake? The curtain covering the entrance to the sanctuary in the Temple was torn. Rocks split. Curious phenomena, not unparalleled at Jerusalem; in 1927 a seismic shock cracked the dome of the Church of the Holy Sepulchre. The dead even appeared at various places in the city. "Heaven and earth," said the prophet Joel, "quake at the sound" (3. 16). Such indeed was the day on which God died.

It is doubtful whether the witnesses of these events realized their significance. Very few could have seen any connection between these apocalyptic phenomena and the end of the paltry agitator who had just died on a bare hillock outside the gate of Ephraim. According to St Matthew (27. 54), one man alone was shaken to the core of his being and converted, the centurion on duty at the place of execution. Perhaps he remembered the phrase used by the Jewish leaders, "He called himself the Son of God", for he exclaimed, "This man was truly the Son of God." The blood shed on the Cross had just made the first conversion to the Christian faith.

Some two hours later the Sabbath of the Passover would begin. The blasts of the ritual trumpet and the lament of the *sophar,* a horn with a sad, grave note, could be heard echoing in the Temple. The Law said that the body of a condemned man was not to be left hanging on a cross through the night, and this was the holy night of the paschal Sabbath. Jesus' body had to be taken down from the cross. The authorization of the Roman Procurator was required. A member of the Sanhedrin—one of those, explains St Luke, who had taken no part in the plans and decisions of the majority (24. 51)—made it his business to go and ask for it. His name was Joseph, and he came from the little town of Arimathea, near Lydda. Together with Nicodemus, he provides clear proof that, even in the governing circles of Israel, the authors of the catastrophe, there were men who were free of any reproach. Some Jews, for quite different motives—they wished to remove the stain from their city—made a similar request at the same time.

Before granting the requested permission Pilate took one precaution. Were the condemned men really dead? A squad of soldiers was sent to see. The two thieves crucified with Jesus were still breathing; their legs were broken with blows from an iron bar to hasten the end. But Jesus was really dead. A soldier mechanically stuck the point of his lance into Jesus' side. "Blood and water flowed out," says St John, who witnessed the scene (19. 32–5). Tradition was to accord a symbolic value to this water and blood, emblems of the baptism and martyrdom both of which redeem. The lance-blow added nothing to the horror of the punishment, but it was certainly true that the piercing of the Son of Man's side had a mystical significance.

So permission was given for Jesus to be taken down from his cross and for his body to be returned to his family and his friends. Before night fell the sad task had been carried out; so too had the formalities of Jewish burial, the washing of the body, the anointing and the wrapping in linen cloths. The obligation to carry out these duties was so categorical that it was permissible to attend to them even on the Sabbath. Then Jesus could be laid in a tomb. Joseph, the councillor from Arimathea, who behaved with decided generosity throughout the whole affair, put at the disposal of Jesus' friends a new tomb which he had had constructed for his own burial (Matt. 27. 60; Mark 15. 42; Luke 23. 50; John 19. 38).

Another influential man also showed his admiration for Jesus; this was Nicodemus, the man who had come to converse with Jesus by night. Christ's words had stirred him, but he had not dared to obey the call. The events which had just taken place had transformed him, and it was he who brought the aromatic spices—myrrh and agalloch[3]—with which custom demanded that the body for burial should be anointed.

Then the stone was rolled up along its grooves to block the entrance to the little corridor which, in the tombs of wealthy Jews, ran into the rock of the hillside and led to the funeral chamber where the body would rest on a stone bench. So the living God lay there, under the ground, wrapped in a shroud, his face veiled, just like a man; and for ever.

[3] Not medicinal aloes, with its noisome smell, as some translations imply.

CHAPTER XX

DEATH, WHERE IS THY VICTORY?

For ever.... That was certainly the conviction of the two men who, on the Sunday evening, were returning home to their village of Emmaus about seven miles from Jerusalem. They were disciples of Jesus, two obscure members of the faithful little band. They walked sadly, ruminating on their disappointment, their bitter sorrow. The great adventure was really over.

While they were talking, a man joined them and walked along with them. Either the shadows of evening or some supernatural power must have prevented them from seeing clearly; at any rate, they did not recognize the stranger. "You look very sad," he said to them, "what's the matter?" One of the two disciples—his name was Cleophas—replied: "Don't you know what has happened at Jerusalem?" "What?" asked the stranger. "The business of Jesus of Nazareth. He was a great prophet in word and deed. The chief priests and the magistrates have had him condemned to death and crucified. We were hoping that he would be the liberator of Israel. As a matter of fact, some women have told an amazing story about an empty tomb and angels appearing to say that he was alive, but we have not seen him."

"Are you so obtuse, then?" replied the stranger. "Have you so little belief in the words of the prophets? Do you not know that it has been said that the Messias would have to suffer in order to enter into his glory?" And quoting continually from the Scriptures he began to explain to them why everything had to happen as it did.

The two disciples began to have a strange feeling; as they listened to him speaking they experienced a sort of deep, mysterious joy, a warmth in their hearts. So when they reached their village—night was falling—they invited the stranger to stay with them. He accepted their invitation, sat down at their table, and, in accordance with custom, took the bread to pronounce the words of benediction; then he broke the bread and gave it to them. At that moment their eyes were opened. A great thrill of joy ran through them; they were speechless with astonishment. It was he! But already he had disappeared again, as suddenly as he had appeared on the road (Luke 24. 13–32; Mark 16. 12).

So the women were right. As soon as the Sabbath, when nothing could be done, was over, they had gone up to Golgotha, in the bright dawn of the Sunday morning, carrying aromatic spices with which to complete their attentions to the body; they had probably had to work too hurriedly on the Friday evening. Who were these brave and dedicated women? Mary of Magdala, she who had poured ointment on Jesus' feet and then followed him devotedly; another Mary, the mother of James, Salome, and Joan, the wife of an official; perhaps five or six altogether. As they walked along, they said to each other: "Who will roll away the stone that closes the entrance to the tomb? It is so heavy."

But when they arrived at the sepulchre, they were amazed. The stone had been rolled out of its grooves. What had happened? Had there been a second earthquake, like the one on Friday? Was that perhaps the rumbling which they had heard as they came up? They had glanced into the funeral chamber; it was empty! What had happened? What power had caused the flight of the soldiers posted at the entrance to the tomb by Pilate to prevent the followers of Jesus from taking away his body secretly? There were no guards there any longer; they had disappeared!

Immediately, Mary Magdalen had run off impetuously towards the gate of the city, and rushed down the steps of the streets with sandals clattering. The Apostles were still in hiding, probably in the poor district of Tyropeon; she knew where they were. Overcome with excitement, she had told them the news. At first they had refused to believe it: "Nonsense! Women's tales!" But she had been so categorical, so positive, that Peter and John had set off for Golgotha. When they had arrived there, they had found that all that Mary Magdalen had told them was true. The stone had really been rolled away; the tomb was really empty. And the other women, who had stayed there, had had a still more amazing experience. Two human forms of dazzling brightness—two angels—had appeared to them and they had heard ineffable voices saying to them: "Why do you seek among the dead him who is alive? He is not here; he has risen again. Do you remember what he told you in days gone by in Galilee: 'The Son of Man must be delivered into the hands of sinners, he must be crucified, but on the third day he will rise again'." (Matt. 28; Mark 16; Luke 23; John 20).

So Jesus had risen again. What can John, the holy women and the others have felt when they were confronted with this marvellous fact? One of them had been so overcome that she had stayed there, weeping with emotion. It was the sinner of Magdala, to whom much had been forgiven because she had loved much. She too had had an angelic vision. The mysterious visitors had questioned her about the cause of her emotion. And at the same moment she had seen a man at her side; through the mist of tears she had not recognized him. But this man had spoken; he had said one single word, "Mary". And she, overcome, pierced to the bottom of her heart, had recognized the voice. It was his voice!

What could she answer? Running towards him, she had stammered, "Master!" What more was there to say or know?

Jesus, who had been crucified, was there, before her. He had called her by her name (John 20. 11–17; Mark 16. 9).

This event, the resurrection of a man who had been dead and buried, is clearly, to the human reason, among the most astonishing events recorded and the most difficult of all to accept. At first sight, it seems as if only an act of faith can enable us to believe in the reality of facts as stupefying as these. However, they are reported by the four evangelists in the same way, in the same tone as the rest of the story of Christ Jesus; and this fourfold witness is also confirmed by the Acts of the Apostles and various passages in the epistles of St Paul, not to mention numerous apocrypha. So it is not because the Creed obliges them to do so that Christians believe that "he rose again from the dead"; on the contrary, they believe unreservedly in the resurrection of Christ because it is an irrefutable fact.

Nevertheless, the fact is such a marvellous one, so contrary to anything in our experience, that ever since it has been known all kinds of theories have been put forward to try to account for it. One suggestion is that Jesus was not really dead. Not dead? After a flogging, the perforation of his hands and feet, hanging for three hours on the Cross and a thrust from a lance right in the heart? To make this hypothesis tenable, all the facts reported by the gospels would have to be false from first to last. And then, as Renan pointed out, the best guarantee that Jesus was really dead when he was taken down from the cross is surely "the suspicious hatred" of the Jewish authorities.

Let us assume that he was dead. Could his body not have been removed by his supporters in order to make people believe that there had been a miracle? This hypothesis seemed so likely that the leaders of the Jewish community hastened to spread just such a rumour, ordering even the guards who had kept watch to accredit it by admitting that they had gone to sleep and that the deed could have been done while they were sleeping (Matt. 28. 12). But the guards were in fact there;

there is no reason to suppose that they did not do their job properly, and even if they had drowsed off it is difficult to see how Jesus' disciples could have rolled the heavy stone sealing the tomb out of its grooves and made it fall without awakening any of them.

Was the sudden reappearance of Christ the result of a collective hallucination—which must have been repeated many times in the course of the period during which the risen Christ showed himself to his followers—or was it a psychical phenomenon of the sort recorded here and there in Scripture? A good example is the evocation of Samuel before Saul by the witch of Endor. But all the details recorded in connection with this "second life" of Jesus contradict this hypothesis, as we shall see. A being who is seen to eat and drink, and whom one can touch, is hardly a hallucination or an ectoplasm!

There remains the hypothesis of a huge piece of deceit, perhaps involuntary; according to this theory, by dint of saying "He cannot be dead" Christ's disciples finished up by asserting, "He has overcome death! He has risen again!" Renan, in a very attractive passage, suggests that it was love, his disciples' love, and above all that of Mary Magdalen, which really "resurrected" Jesus. Guignebert has taken the idea up and developed it, suggesting that it was the first Christians who not only made Jesus into the Messias, the Son of God, but also proclaimed that he had lived after death. In this case, everything is just a magnificent story. One feels inclined to counter this theory with Renan's own very pertinent remarks: "Nothing lasts except the truth.... All that serves it is preserved like a small but solid piece of capital; nothing of the tiny sum is lost. What is false, on the other hand, crumbles away. The false cannot serve as a foundation for anything; while the tiny edifice of truth is made of steel, and is always rising higher."[1] After twenty centuries, the mere presence of the Christian faith in millions of souls would seem to be the most decisive argument.

[1] *History of the People of Israel*, p. 421.

Jesus' "second life", his life after death, lasted forty days. This "forty days" is a mystical period; it is the period of John's retreat into the desert, of Moses' sojourn on Sinai, and of the Christian Lent. Events are recorded by the evangelists in such a way that it is difficult to make a connected narrative of them. It is as if, in this story which is in any case supernatural, each of them had noted certain points which had struck him particularly, which seemed highly charged with significance.

For forty days, then, Jesus was among his followers again, and on many occasions he behaved like a man who was very much alive and perfectly real. To his disciples, dismayed by his sudden appearance, he said: "Look at me, touch me. A ghost has neither flesh nor bones as I have." Then, to convince them finally, he asked for food and shared with them the fish from the lake which they had just grilled (Luke 24. 36–43). The famous episode of Thomas, the incredulous Apostle, is still more significant; he had not been a witness of the first appearances of the Risen Christ and had absolutely refused to believe the assertions of his comrades, but Christ rose up before him, reproached him with his incredulity, and commanded him to touch the wounds in his hands and side. A ghost does not possess a body that one can touch with one's finger (John 20. 24–9).

Nevertheless, it is clear that many aspects of this "second life" are disconcerting, inexplicable in any rational fashion, and more akin to psychical than physical laws. Already on Easter morning Jesus had said to Mary Magdalen: "Do not cling to me thus, I have not yet gone up to my Father's side." What do these enigmatic words mean? Why did several of those who saw him at close quarters not recognize him? This happened with Mary Magdalen, with the disciples from Emmaus, and with the Apostles themselves when they met him on the shore of the Sea of Galilee (John 21. 4). Stranger still, he appears and disappears suddenly, as we have seen in the Emmaus incident, and he even passes through the closed doors of the room in which his followers are assembled (Luke 24. 36; John 20. 19). We have to acknowledge, then, that during these forty days Christ was as real as a man of flesh and blood, yet his body enjoyed supernatural gifts which cannot belong to earth. What St Paul was to call, in the First Epistle to the Corinthians, the "spiritual body" finds here its first example and its archetype.

For the rest, the attitude of the risen Christ is identical with that of the living one. His teaching takes up its earlier themes, almost word for word, and he presides over a miraculous draught of fishes as he had done once before. He recalls the great truths of his message, especially that of the primacy of love. He confirms Simon Peter's commission to "feed his sheep", that is, guide the Church (John 21. 15–17). Above all, to all those who hear him, and to all those who were to hear him in the future through the words of his followers, he gives an order and he makes a promise. The order is "Go and teach all nations", that is, "Be apostles yourselves". The promise is the one which Christians will cherish to the last day as the guarantee of their hope: "I am with you all through the days that are coming, until the consummation of the world" (Matt. 28. 18–20; Mark 16. 15–19).

So ended, with a mysterious but promise-laden chapter, finally closed by the mystical apotheosis of the Ascension, the earthly life of Jesus Christ. How often had he not foretold his Resurrection, which was an integral part of his Passion and gave it its whole meaning! Those who had followed him since the start of his mission now understood statements of his which, at the time, had astonished and shocked them, statements such as "The Son of Man must be handed over to his enemies, he must suffer, die on the cross and afterwards rise again", or again—the play on words has something so shocking about it that one can forgive the disciples for not understanding it—"When I have been lifted up, I will attract all men to myself." Henceforth everything was to appear clear, logical and providential.

The Resurrection proved that it was all true, that Jesus was truly God incarnate, the Son of God, the Messias, that he had indeed come on earth to ensure men's salvation by his sacrifice, and that the way he had shown them was the only one to follow. This is what St Paul, that inspired interpreter of Christ's message, was to make so wonderfully clear. On the one hand he was to show that the fact of the Resurrection was the cornerstone of Christianity: "If Christ has not risen, ... if the hope we have learned to repose in Christ belongs to this world only, then we are unhappy beyond all other men" (1 Cor. 15. 14, 19). On the other, he asserted that Christ's victory over death forms a glorious conclusion to his struggle to save humanity from evil and sin: "Death, where is thy victory? Death, where is thy sting? It is sin that gives death its sting" (1 Cor. 15. 55–7).

It was this faith in Jesus Christ, God made man, freely offered up to deliver humanity from sin and death, and then risen again, that the first disciples, the first Christians felt beating within them in time with their hearts when one day in May, on the Mount of Olives, they saw their Master disappear into Heaven. That is the message which, strengthened by the Holy Spirit, and in accordance with Christ's command, they were to hand down to all men from century to century. Indeed, it was more than a message; it was a presence, the sweetest, most radiant of all presences; twenty centuries have not dimmed its splendour or the mysterious hold which it exerts on men's souls. Jesus Christ is there, for all those who love him and follow him; more alive than any living person, near at hand, real, deeper within a man than his own soul. So it will be "until the consummation of the world", as Christ himself has said.

CHRONOLOGICAL TABLE

In June: Jesus goes to Jerusalem; the healing of the paralytic at the pool.

In July: Jesus says to Peter: "Thou art Peter and on this rock. . . ."

In August: The Transfiguration and predictions of the Passion.

In September: Jesus moves from Galilee to Judaea.

In October: The Feast of Tents (Tabernacles); episode of the woman taken in adultery. Parable of the Good Samaritan. Mary and Martha at Bethany.

In December: The debate with the Pharisees grows lively.

30 *In January:* The Parables of Mercy (the strayed sheep, the lost groat, the prodigal son).

In March: The raising of Lazarus; the anger of Jesus' opponents increases. The episode of Zacchaeus the publican. The meal at Bethany and the anointing of Christ by Mary.

Holy Week (in the year 30).

Sunday, April 2nd: Triumphal entry.

Monday, 3rd: The cursing of the fig-tree; the parables of warning (the murderous vine-dressers).

Tuesday, 4th: Jesus repels the attacks of his opponents. He prophesies the destruction of Jerusalem and the Last Judgement.

Wednesday, 5th: The treachery of Judas.

Thursday, 6th: The Last Supper and the institution of the Eucharist.

Night of 6th to 7th: The "Trial" of Jesus.

Friday, 7th: The Passion and crucifixion of Jesus.

Sunday, 9th: The tomb of Christ is found to be empty; Jesus rises again.

Forty days later: The Ascension.

Ten days later still: Pentecost; the Holy Spirit gives the Apostles the strength to bear witness to the death and resurrection of Christ. The Church of Christ begins.

SELECT BIBLIOGRAPHY

In this series: AMIOT, François, P.S.S., BRUNOT, Amédée, S.C.J., DANIÉLOU, Jean, S.J., DANIEL-ROPS: *The Sources for the Life of Christ*; DANIEL-ROPS: *What is the Bible?* PAUPERT, J. M.: *What is the Gospel?* STEINMANN, Jean: *Biblical Criticism.*

ADAM, Karl: *The Son of God,* London, Burns and Oates, 1938, and New York, Sheed and Ward, 1940.

DANIEL-ROPS: *Jesus and His Times,* New York, Dutton, 1954, and London, Burns and Oats, 1955; *Daily Life in the Time of Jesus,* New York, Hawthorn Books, and London, Weidenfeld, 1962.

GRANDMAISON, L. de, S.J.: *Jesus Christ, His Person, His Life, His Credentials,* London, Sheed and Ward, 1935.

GROLLENBERG, L. H., O.P.: *Atlas of the Bible,* translated and edited by H. H. Rowley and Joyce M. H. Reid, London and New York, Nelson, 1956.

GUARDINI, Romano: *The Lord,* London and New York, Longmans, 1956.

GUITTON, Jean: *The Problem of Jesus,* London, Burns and Oates, and New York, Kenedy, 1955.

JOHNSTON, L., and PICKERING, A. (Editors): *A Harmony of the Gospels in the Knox Translation,* London, Burns and Oates, and New York, Sheed and Ward, 1963.

KEE, H. C., and YOUNG, F. W.: *Understanding the New Testament,* New York, Prentice Hall, 1957 (English edn, *Living World of the New Testament,* London, Darton, Longman and Todd, 1960).

KLEIST, James A., S.J.: *New Testament,* Milwaukee, Bruce, 1954.

KNOX, R. A.: *New Testament Commentary for English Readers,* three volumes, London, Burns and Oates, and New York, Sheed and Ward, 1953–6.

LAGRANGE, M. J.: *A Catholic Harmony of the Gospels,* adapted by J. M. T. Barton, London, Burns and Oates, 1936; *The Gospel of Jesus Christ,* London, Burns and Oates, and Westminster, Md, Newman Press, 1943.

LATTEY, C., S.J.: *The New Testament in the Westminster Version,* London and New York, Longmans, 1937.

LEBRETON, J.: *The Life and Teaching of Jesus Christ*, revised edn, London, Burns and Oates, and New York, Macmillan, 1935; *The Spiritual Teaching of the New Testament*, London, Burns and Oates, 1960.

MORTON, H. V.: *In the Steps of the Master*, London, Methuen, and New York, Dodd, 1934.